COMMON CORE ACHIEVE

Mastering Essential Test Readiness Skills

TASC Test Exercise Book

MATHEMATICS

Mc
Graw
Hill
Education

Bothell, WA • Chicago, IL • Columbus, OH • New York, NY

MHEonline.com

Send all inquiries to:
McGraw-Hill Education
8787 Orion Place
Columbus, OH 43240

ISBN: 978-0-02-143261-5
MHID: 0-02-143261-9

Printed in the United States of America.

3 4 5 6 7 8 9 RHR 17 16 15 14

Table of Contents

Congratulations! If you are using this book, it means that you are taking a key step toward achieving an important new goal for yourself. You are preparing to take the TASC Test Assessing Secondary Completion™, one of the most important steps in the pathway toward career, educational, and lifelong well-being and success.

Common Core Achieve: Mastering Essential Test Readiness Skills is designed to help you learn or strengthen the skills you will need when you take the TASC test. The Mathematics Exercise Book provides you with additional practice of the key concepts, core skills, and core practices required for success on test day and beyond.

How to Use This Book

This book is designed to follow the same lesson structure as the Core Student Module. Each lesson in the Mathematics Exercise Book is broken down into the same sections as the core module, with a page or more devoted to the key concepts covered in each section. Each lesson contains at least one Test-Taking Tip, which will help you prepare for a test by giving you strategies for how to approach multiple choice or gridded response questions, or tips for using charts, graphs, or other information to answer questions. At the back of this book, you will find the answer key for each lesson. The answer to each question is provided along with a rationale for why the answer is correct. If you get an answer incorrect, please return to the appropriate lesson and section in either the online or print Core Student Module to review the specific content.

A Mathematical Formulas sheet is provided at the back of this book that lists all of the formulas you will need while working on the lessons. In addition, there is a TASC Test Mathematics Reference Sheet which lists the formulas that are available during the test.

About the TASC Test for Mathematics

The TASC test for Mathematics assesses across five content categories (approximate percentage of test questions in each category is shown in parenthesis): Number and Quantity (15%), Geometry (25%), Statistics and Probability (10%), Algebra (25%), and Measurement Functions (25%). The test is divided into two parts: Part 1 is 55 minutes and Part 2 is 50 minutes. Students are permitted to use a calculator for Part 2 but not for Part 1.

Questions are primarily multiple choice; however, there are gridded response items for a small number of questions. As you work through the lessons in this book, you will practice using the gridded response item format.

Strategies for Test Day

There are many things you should do to prepare for test day, including studying. Other ways to prepare you for the day of the test include preparing physically, arriving early, and recognizing certain strategies to help you succeed during the test. Some of these strategies are listed below.

- **Prepare physically.** Make sure you are rested both physically and mentally the day of the test. Eating a well-balanced meal will also help you concentrate while taking the test. Staying stress-free as much as possible on the day of the test will make you more likely to stay focused than when you are stressed.

- **Arrive early.** Arrive at the testing center at least 30 minutes before the beginning of the test. Give yourself enough time to get seated and situated in the room. Keep in mind that some testing centers will not admit you if you are late.

- **Think positively.** Studies have shown that a positive attitude can help with success, although studying helps even more.

- **Relax during the test.** Stretching and deep breathing can help you relax and refocus. Try doing this a few times during the test, especially if you feel frustrated, anxious, or confused.

- **Read the test directions carefully.** Make sure you understand what the directions are asking you to do and complete the activity appropriately. If you have any questions about the test, or how to answer a specific item type using the computer, ask before the beginning of the test.

- **Have a strategy for answering questions.** For each question, read the question promptly, identifying the most important information needed to answer the question. If necessary, reread the supporting information provided as well as the answer choices provided.

- **Don't spend a lot of time on difficult questions.** If you are unable to answer a question or are not confident in your answer, move on and come back to it later. If you are taking the paper and pencil version of the TASC test, mark your test booklet so you can easily find questions you have skipped. If you are taking the computer-based version of the TASC test, the testing software includes a tool that allows you to mark questions and move on to the next question. Answer easier questions first. If time permits at the end of the test, go back and review and answer questions you have marked. Regardless of whether you have skipped questions or not, try to finish with around 10–15 minutes left so you have time to check some of your answers.

- **Answer every question on the test.** If you do not know the answer, make your best guess. You will lose points leaving questions unanswered, but making a guess could possibly help you gain points.

Good luck with your studies, and remember: you are here because you have chosen to achieve important and exciting new goals for yourself. Every time you begin working within the materials, keep in mind that the skills you develop in *Common Core Achieve: Mastering Essential Test Readiness Skills* are not just important for passing the TASC test; they are keys to lifelong success.

This lesson will help you practice ordering and comparing numbers. Use it with Core Lesson 1.1 *Order Rational Numbers* to reinforce and apply your knowledge.

Key Concept

Rational numbers include whole numbers, fractions, decimals, and their opposites. A number line is a useful math tool for comparing and ordering rational numbers.

Core Skills

- Use Math Tools Appropriately
- Apply Number Sense

Rational Numbers

We rely on rational numbers to count, measure, and describe situations each day.

Directions: Answer the questions below.

1. **Look at this number line.**

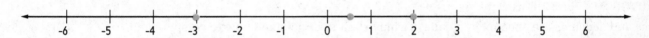

    Select the rational numbers that are marked on the number line above.

    A $-1, 3, 5$

    B $-3, \frac{1}{2}, 2$

    C $-1, -\frac{1}{2}, 3$

    D $-3, \frac{3}{4}, 2$

2. **Which option best explains why the product of rational numbers is rational?**

    F You can rewrite $a(b + c)$ as $ab + ac$ and get the same answer because multiplication can be distributed over addition.

    G The product $(a \times b) \times c$ can be rewritten as $a \times (b \times c)$ because the way you group rational numbers when multiplying does not matter.

    H $a \times b \times c = y$ is the same as $b \times a \times c = y$ when a, b, and c are whole-number integers because the order in which rational numbers are multiplied does not change the product.

    J In the equation $\frac{a}{b} \times \frac{c}{d} = \frac{a \times c}{b \times d}$, if a, b, c, and d are integers then the product is a rational number because all rational numbers can be written as an integer divided by another integer.

3. **What property do irrational numbers have?**

   A They have perfect squares.

   B They include the set of all whole numbers.

   C They cannot be expressed as the ratio of two integers.

   D They are terminating decimals that do not repeat.

4. **Compare $\sqrt{2}$ and $\sqrt{1}$; which number is rational and why?**

   F $\sqrt{2}$; 2 is a perfect square.

   G $\sqrt{1}$; 1 is a perfect square.

   H $\sqrt{2}$; it's an infinite decimal.

   J $\sqrt{1}$; it's an infinite decimal.

Fractions and Decimals

Fractions and decimals are encountered daily; it's important to understand how to compare and order them.

Directions: Answer the questions below.

5. **A runner logs her runs using a phone. The table below shows her distances for five days. Which list of numbers shows the correct order from shortest to longest?**

Mon	Tues	Wed	Thurs	Fri
$2\frac{6}{10}$	$2\frac{3}{12}$	$2\frac{3}{4}$	$2\frac{3}{8}$	$2\frac{6}{9}$

   A $2\frac{3}{4}$, $2\frac{3}{8}$, $2\frac{3}{12}$, $2\frac{6}{9}$, $2\frac{6}{10}$

   B $2\frac{3}{12}$, $2\frac{3}{8}$, $2\frac{3}{4}$, $2\frac{6}{10}$, $2\frac{6}{9}$

   C $2\frac{3}{12}$, $2\frac{3}{8}$, $2\frac{6}{10}$, $2\frac{6}{9}$, $2\frac{3}{4}$

   D $2\frac{3}{4}$, $2\frac{6}{9}$, $2\frac{6}{10}$, $2\frac{3}{8}$, $2\frac{3}{10}$

✓ Test-Taking Tip

Each of the mixed numbers in the problem above has different denominators. Therefore, it is difficult to list them in order without first converting each mixed number to equal terms or to decimal numbers. Test problems such as this, as well as measurement problems that include different units of measurement (yards, feet, and inches), often use quantities that must be converted in one way or another before comparing them or using them in calculations. It is important to always verify that the information provided in a problem does not need to be converted before solving the problem.

6. **Which of these numbers is the largest? Please enter your response in the grid.**

10.02

10.26

10.5

10.23

7. **Which number represents $\frac{28}{5}$ as a mixed number?**

   A $5\frac{3}{5}$

   B $5\frac{2}{3}$

   C $7\frac{2}{5}$

   D $7\frac{3}{5}$

8. **Which number represents $\frac{47}{3}$ as a mixed number?**

   F $15\frac{2}{3}$

   G $15\frac{2}{5}$

   H $15\frac{2}{3}$

   J $16\frac{1}{3}$

9. **Which of these numbers is the smallest?**

   A 7.45

   B 7.75

   C $7\frac{3}{8}$

   D $7\frac{4}{5}$

Absolute Value

Absolute value describes the distance a number is from zero.

Directions: Answer the questions below.

10. Look at this number line.

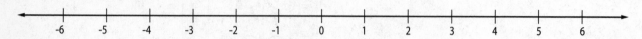

Which numbers are within a distance of 3 units from the number 2?

F −1, 5

G −3, 9

H −1, 9

J −3, 5

11. What is the distance between −6 and 3?

A −9

B −3

C 3

D 9

12. What is the absolute value of the sum of −17 + 8?

F −9

G 9

H 11

J 25

13. At the warehouse where you work, you are in charge of the inventory. The warehouse has 217 gym bags in stock. You receive an order for 538 bags. How many bags are now on back order?

A −755

B −321

C 321

D 755

This lesson will help you practice adding, subtracting, multiplying, and dividing rational numbers. Use it with Core Lesson 1.2 *Apply Number Properties* to reinforce and apply your knowledge.

Key Concept

The least common multiple and greatest common factor of a pair of numbers can be used to solve problems. Awareness of number properties can be helpful in evaluating numerical expressions, although some expressions are undefined.

Core Skills

- Apply Number Sense Concepts
- Perform Operations

Factors and Multiples

You can use the concepts of factors and multiples to figure out how to break up a number of items into smaller groups or to determine how many items you will need to complete a task.

Directions: Answer the questions below.

1. **Consider this tree diagram.**

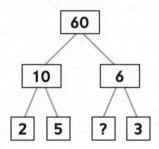

   Which of these is the unknown number?

   A 2

   B 3

   C 5

   D 7

2. **Which expression shows the prime factorization of 60?**

   F $2^2 \times 3^2 \times 5$

   G $2 \times 3^2 \times 5^2$

   H $2^2 \times 3 \times 5$

   J $2 \times 3^2 \times 5$

3. There are 20 distance runners and 25 sprinters in a running club. The head of the club wants to organize the club members into equal-sized groups. Each group will have the same number of distance runners and sprinters. Which explanation correctly demonstrates why there will be 9 people in each group?

A $25 + 20 = 45$ and $25 - 20 = 5$. Dividing 45 by 5 gives 9 people in each group.

B There will be 5 people in each group since the greatest common factor of 20 and 25 is 5.

C The number of groups is 5 because $25 - 20 = 5$. There will be 4 distance runners and 5 sprinters in each group, a total of 9.

D The number of groups is 5 because the greatest common factor of 20 and 25 is 5. There will be 4 distance runners and 5 sprinters in each group, a total of 9.

4. A craftsman purchases materials to make dog collars for a pet shop. There are 12 buckles in a pack and 16 straps in a pack. What is the least number of packs of buckles and straps the craftsman should buy so there are no supplies left over?

F 1 pack of buckles and 1 pack of straps

G 2 packs of buckles and 1 pack of straps

H 4 packs of buckles and 3 packs of straps

J 16 packs of buckles and 12 packs of straps

5. An artist is making a small sketch based on a 12-inch by 30-inch poster. She divides the poster into equal-sized grid squares to make it easier to resize. What is the area, in square inches, of the largest grid squares she can make to cover the poster? Please enter your response in the grid.

Test-Taking Tip

When you enter your responses in the gridded area on the test, don't leave any blank columns between numbers and symbols. For example, if your answer has 3 numbers and a decimal point, then you should have 4 columns in a row filled in.

Properties of Numbers

There are certain properties of numbers you can use to help make your calculations easier.

Directions: Answer the questions below.

6. **Consider this equation.**

$$2(6 + 3) = 2 \times 6 + \underline{\hspace{1cm}}$$

Which expression completes the equation?

F 2×3

G $2 + 3$

H 2×6

J $2 + 6$

7. **Which equation illustrates the Commutative Property of Addition?**

A $x + 0 = x$

B $x + y = y + x$

C $x(y + z) = xy + xz$

D $x + (y + z) = (x + y) + z$

8. **Consider the table below that shows the number of tee shirts sold by four vendors at a concert this weekend.**

	Vendor A	Vendor B	Vendor C	Vendor D
Friday	85	101	65	22
Saturday	101	92	77	19
Sunday	92	85	83	12

Which of these statements is true?

F Vendor A sold more total shirts than Vendor B.

G Vendor B sold fewer total shirts than Vendor C.

H Vendor B sold more total shirts than Vendors C and D combined.

J Vendor A sold the same number of total shirts as Vendor C and D combined.

9. **Consider this equation.**

   $5 \times 35 = 5 \times 20 + \underline{\hspace{1cm}} \times 15$

   What number correctly completes the equation? Please enter your response in the grid.

10. **Naomi has a red box. The red box is 9 inches long, 6 inches wide, and 2 inches tall. She is going to order a blue box that has the same volume as the red box, but not the same size. Which process guarantees that her blue box will have the same volume?**

    F Triple the height and one-third the length.

    G Double all of the dimensions of the red box.

    H Find 3 numbers that add up to $9 + 6 + 2 = 17$.

    J Add 2 inches to the width and subtract 2 inches from the length.

✔ **Test-Taking Tip**

The answer choices for multiple-choice problems may contain numbers from the problem as a means of distraction. However, sometimes they—along with a property of numbers—are exactly what you need in order to solve a problem and avoid having to make unnecessary calculations.

8

Order of Operations

When evaluating expressions, the order in which different operations are performed has a direct impact on the final answer, so rules and conventions must be followed.

Directions: Answer the questions below.

11. **Marci wrote this expression.**

    $20 \div (49 - m^2)$

    What positive number m makes this expression undefined? Please enter your response in the grid.

12. **Suppose that 100 is the best possible score on a test, and any score over 70 is considered a passing grade. Which expression is equal to a passing grade on the test?**

    F $100 - \dfrac{5}{2} \times 20$

    G $100 - \dfrac{12}{2} \times 5$

    H $100 - \dfrac{5}{2} \times 10$

    J $100 - \dfrac{12}{2} \times 15$

13. **Kevin made an error while evaluating the expression below.**

    $2(16 \div (8 - 6)^3 + 5)$
    $2(2 - 216 + 5)$
    $2(-209)$
    -418

    Which of these should he do to correct his error?

    A Work in order from left to right to add and subtract; then multiply and divide.

    B Perform operations outside the parentheses first; then work from left to right.

    C Do the operation in the inner set of parentheses before evaluating the exponent.

    D Work in order from right to left to multiply and divide; then evaluate the exponent.

14. Marcie buys 3 shirts at $15 each. She also buys a $30 jacket that is on sale at a $5 discount. She uses a $10 gift card towards her purchase. Which expression shows how much Marcie spends?

F $(3 \times 15 + (30 - 5)) - 10$

G $(3 \times 15 + (30 - 5)) + 10$

H $(3 + 15 + (30 - 5)) - 10$

J $(3 + 15 + (30 - 5)) + 10$

15. Which expression has a value of 21?

A $(5 + 6)^2 - \dfrac{10}{2} + 3$

B $5 + \dfrac{(6^2 - 10)}{2} + 3$

C $5 + 6^2 - \left(\dfrac{10}{2}\right) + 3$

D $5 + 6^2 - \dfrac{10}{(2 + 3)}$

16. Consider this expression.

$$\dfrac{15 + \left(\dfrac{36}{9} - 8 \times 3 + 25\right)^2}{6 + 4}$$

Which statement explains which step must come first in the order of operations to simplify the expression?

F The numbers $\dfrac{36}{9} - 8 \times 3 + 25$ must be squared.

G The number 15 must be added to $\dfrac{36}{9} - 8 \times 3 + 25$.

H The number $\dfrac{36}{9}$ must be replaced with 4.

J The numbers $6 + 4$ must be replaced with 10.

This lesson will help you practice using exponents and scientific notation to solve real-world problems. Use it with Core Lesson 1.3 *Compute with Exponents* to reinforce and apply your knowledge.

Key Concept

Exponents can be used to represent and solve problems, such as those involving squares and cubes or scientific notation. You can use the rules of exponents to rewrite and simplify expressions involving exponents.

Core Skills

* Represent Real-World Problems
* Make Use of Structure

Exponential Notation

Exponential notation is a way to express repeated multiplication. It is useful for computing investments and measuring areas.

Directions: Answer the questions below.

1. Ceramic tile costs $2.50 per square foot, and the installation fee for one room of tile is $175. Which expression can be used to find the total cost of installing ceramic tile in a room that is 14 feet by 14 feet?

    A $2.50^2 \times 14 + 175$

    B $2.50 \times 14^2 + 175$

    C $2.50 \times 14 + 175^2$

    D $2.50^2 \times 14^2 + 175$

2. What is the value of the expression $x^2 + y^3$ for $x = 4$ and $y = 2$? Please enter your response in the grid.

3. Consider the table below that shows the cost of sod at four different garden shops.

Garden Shop	Sod Cost per Square Foot
A	$0.40
B	$0.50
C	$0.60
D	$0.70

Which of these purchases is the most expensive?

A   sod purchased from Shop A to cover 20 ft by 20 ft

B   sod purchased from Shop B to cover 16 ft by 16 ft

C   sod purchased from Shop C to cover 18 ft by 18 ft

D   sod purchased from Shop D to cover 15 ft by 15 ft

4. Juan is planting flower seeds in 6 large cubic containers and 1 small cubic container. The side length of each large container measures 4 inches, and the side length of the small container measures 3 inches. Which expression represents the number of cubic inches of dirt Juan will need to completely fill all the containers with soil?

F $6 \times 4^3 + 3^3$

G $6 \times 4^2 + 3^2$

H $6 \times 4^3 + 1 + 3^3$

J $6 \times 4^2 + 1 + 3^2$

5. What is the value of a if the expression $13y^a + 1 = 14$ for all y? Please enter your response in the grid.

Test-Taking Tip

When you enter your responses in the gridded area on the test, you can start your answers in any column as long as all of the digits and symbols fit within the five columns. For example, if you need to enter 5 characters, don't start your answer in the second column. Your answer won't fit, and it will be counted wrong even if you knew the correct answer.

Rules of Exponents

The rules of exponents help you simplify expressions involving exponents and make them easier to solve.

Directions: Answer the questions below.

6. Which property can be used to simplify the expression $(4a^4)^2$?

   F Distributive Property

   G Power of a Power Property

   H Product of Powers Property

   J Quotient of Powers Property

7. Consider this equation.

   $(2^m)^4 = 2^{-12}$

   Which of these is the value of m?

   A $m = -8$

   B $m = -3$

   C $m = 3$

   D $m = 8$

8. Which expression has the least value?

   F $(12^2)^5$

   G $12^2 \times 12^5$

   H $12^5 \div 12^2$

   J $12^{-3} \times 12^4$

9. Which of these has the same value as the expression $(2^2 \times 3^3)^4$?

   A 6^{20}

   B 6^{24}

   C $2^6 \times 3^7$

   D $2^8 \times 3^{12}$

Scientific Notation

Scientific notation simplifies calculations with very small or very large numbers, which is useful for such tasks as computing long distances, measuring small objects, and modeling populations.

Directions: Answer the questions below.

10. Olivia says 65.2×10^5 is the number 6,520,000 written in scientific notation. Which statement explains how she can correct her mistake?

   F She needs to change the exponent to 6.

   G She needs to change the exponent to -5.

   H She needs to change 65.2 to 6.52 and change the exponent to 6.

   J She needs to move the decimal in 65.2 one more place to the left, and keep the exponent as 5.

11. The mass of a particle of dust is 0.0000000504 grams. Which of these is this number expressed in scientific notation?

   A 5.4×10^{-8}

   B 5.04×10^{-8}

   C 50.4×10^{-9}

   D 5.04×10^9

12. A biologist can grow 645,300,000 bacteria in one Petri dish. Which expression gives the number of bacteria she can grow in 10 Petri dishes?

   F 6.453×10^{-9}

   G 6.453×10^{-8}

   H 6.453×10^8

   J 6.453×10^9

13. One container holds 4.2×10^5 particles of sand, and another container holds 6.7×10^3 particles of sand. Which expression, written in correct scientific notation, represents how many total particles of sand are in these two containers?

   A 4.267×10^8

   B 0.4267×10^6

   C 4.267×10^5

   D 42.67×10^4

 **Test-Taking Tip**

When completing a multiple-choice exercise, read all the answer choices carefully before you select your answer. A decimal point or an exponent number can change an answer dramatically.

This lesson will help you practice computing with roots using rules of exponents. Use it with Core Lesson 1.4 *Compute with Roots* to reinforce and apply your knowledge.

Key Concept	Core Skills
Numerical expressions involving roots (often called radicals) can be written using rational exponents and then simplified using the rules of exponents.	• Represent Real-World Arithmetic Problems • Attend to Precision

Square Roots and Cube Roots

Just as you can use squares and cubes to find area and volume, you can use square roots and cube roots to find side lengths from knowing an area or a volume.

Directions: Answer the questions below.

1. **Which statement is true?**

    A The fifth root of 256 is 4.

    B The cube root of 256 is 4.

    C The fourth root of 256 is 4.

    D The square root of 256 is 4.

2. **A restaurant has been using plates with a 10-inch diameter. The manager decides to switch to plates that will hold 50% more food. To the nearest tenth of an inch, what is the diameter of the new plates?**

    F 12.2 in.

    G 13.2 in.

    H 14.4 in.

    J 15 in.

3. **Which of these is sometimes larger than the original number?**

    A cube root of an integer

    B sixth root of an integer

    C fourth root of an integer

    D square root of an integer

4. If a gallon of paint covers 350 square feet (ft²), which of these, to the nearest tenth of a foot, is the side length of the largest square floor space that you could paint with one gallon?

   F 7.0 ft

   G 7.6 ft

   H 18.7 ft

   J 20.0 ft

5. One cubic foot of a swimming pool holds 7.48 gallons of water. Which of these, to the nearest whole foot, is the shortest possible side length of a cubical pool that can hold 10,000 gallons?

   A 10 ft

   B 11 ft

   C 12 ft

   D 13 ft

6. The square root of a positive integer is either an integer or which of these?

   F a prime factor

   G a rational number

   H a rational exponent

   J an irrational number

7. How many feet of fence are required to enclose a square area of 56.25 square feet (ft²)? Please enter your response in the grid.

8. What is the side length, to the nearest whole foot, of a cube that will contain 4,000 cubic feet (ft³)? Please enter your response in the grid.

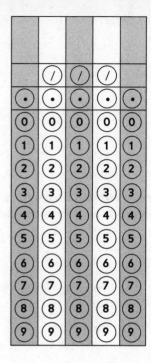

9. A ship owner has a cube of cement 1 ft on a side to be used as an anchor. The ship owner wants another cube of cement twice as heavy as the first one. What will be the side length, to the nearest hundredth of a foot, of the second cube?

A 1.26 ft

B 1.41 ft

C 1.50 ft

D 2 ft

Radicals and Rational Exponents

It can be helpful to simplify radicals if they are in the form of a rational exponent because the rules of exponents can be applied.

Directions: Answer the questions below.

10. A square window has a side length of 1 meter (m). The diagonal measures $\sqrt{2}$ meter. A fly can walk diagonally across the window in 1 minute. To the nearest tenth of a minute, how long will it take the fly to walk around the perimeter of the window?

F 0.7

G 1.4

H 2.8

J 4

11. Which expression does <u>not</u> equal 27?

   A $9^{\frac{3}{2}}$

   B $81^{\frac{3}{4}}$

   C $\sqrt{9^3}$

   D $\sqrt[3]{9^2}$

12. You want to construct a cube-shaped box with a volume of 750 cubic centimeters (cm³). Which expression shows the area, in square centimeters, of one face of the cube?

   F $750^{\frac{2}{3}}$

   G $750^{\frac{3}{2}}$

   H $6\left(750^{\frac{1}{3}}\right)$

   J $\dfrac{750^{\frac{2}{3}}}{6}$

13. Which of these is $\dfrac{\sqrt{96}}{\sqrt{12}}$ simplified?

   A $\dfrac{2}{\sqrt{2}}$

   B $\sqrt{2}$

   C $\sqrt{6}$

   D $2\sqrt{2}$

14. The area of the top of a cube-shaped trash bin is 800 square inches (in²). To the nearest cubic inch, what is the volume of the trash bin?

   F 4,800 in.³

   G 22,627 in.³

   H 2,370,370 in.³

   J 512,000,000 in.³

15. If $\sqrt{\sqrt[3]{x}} = \sqrt[3]{\sqrt{x}}$, what are the possible values for x?

   A Any integer

   B Either 0 or 1

   C No possible values

   D Any nonnegative real number

16. What is $\dfrac{\sqrt[3]{108}(\sqrt[3]{16})}{\sqrt{9}}$ completely simplified?

Please enter your response in the grid.

17. Which of these is $\sqrt{\sqrt[6]{2}}$ simplified completely?

A $\sqrt[12]{2}$

B $\sqrt[8]{2}$

C $\sqrt[3]{2}$

D $2^{\sqrt{6}}$

18. Which of these expressions is equivalent to $\dfrac{\sqrt{40} \times \sqrt[3]{8}}{\sqrt{2}}$

F $\dfrac{2\sqrt{10}(\sqrt[3]{8})}{\sqrt{2}}$

G $\dfrac{10^{\frac{1}{2}} \times 8^{\frac{1}{3}}}{2^{\frac{1}{2}}}$

H $5^{\frac{1}{2}} \times \dfrac{2}{2^{\frac{1}{2}}}$

J $\sqrt{5} \times \dfrac{\sqrt{2}}{2}$

✓ **Test-Taking Tip**

Certain operations with roots are easy to confuse. For instance $x^{\frac{3}{2}}$, is not half of x^3, it is the square root of x^3. The square root of the cube root of 2 is not $2^{\frac{3}{2}}$ but $2^{\frac{1}{6}}$. Think a minute about how root operations work before selecting your answer.

19. Consider Jessica's work for simplifying an expression.

$$\frac{\sqrt{25}}{\sqrt[3]{125}} = \frac{25^{\frac{1}{2}}}{125^{\frac{1}{3}}} = \frac{1^{\frac{1}{2}}}{5^{\frac{1}{3}}} = \frac{1}{\sqrt[3]{5}}$$

What, if any, was her mistake?

A No mistake, her work is correct.

B She divided terms with unequal exponents.

C She should have divided by dividing exponents.

D She should have divided by subtracting exponents.

20. Which number has the least value?

F 7

G $\sqrt[3]{350}$

H $\sqrt{48}$

J $\dfrac{50}{7}$

21. What is the value of $\dfrac{\sqrt[3]{54}(\sqrt[3]{4})}{\sqrt{125}(\sqrt{5})}$ in simplest form?

Please enter your response in the grid.

This lesson will help you practice setting up and calculating with ratios, proportions, and scale factors. Use it with Core Lesson 2.1 *Apply Ratios and Proportions* to reinforce and apply your knowledge.

Key Concept	Core Skills
A ratio, which is often written as a fraction, is a comparison of the relative sizes of two numbers. Operations on ratios follow the same rules as operations on fractions. When two ratios are equivalent, they are called proportional.	• Compare Unit Rates • Use Ratio Reasoning

Ratios

Ratios occur throughout your daily routine, including miles per hour for speed and cost per pound for fruits and vegetables.

Directions: Answer the questions below.

1. There are 500 boys to 120 girls in a college. Which of these ratios of boys to girls is equivalent?

    A $\frac{25}{12}$

    B $\frac{25}{6}$

    C $\frac{50}{9}$

    D $\frac{50}{3}$

2. In a store, screws are sold for $3.48 a pound. You want to buy 7 pounds for one project and 5 pounds for another project. How much will you spend on screws for both projects?

    F $6.96

    G $17.40

    H $24.36

    J $41.76

3. On a farm, there are 24 cows, 16 chickens, 20 horses, and 15 pigs. Which ratio is the greatest?

    A Pigs:Cows

    B Horses:Pigs

    C Cows:Chickens

    D Chickens:Horses

4. One car travels 240 miles in 4 hours while another car travels 275 miles in 5 hours. What is the difference in the rates of speed in miles per hour?

   F 1

   G 5

   H 7

   J 35

5. A brand of vitamin tablets comes in three different sizes of bottles:

Small:	60 tablets for $5.40
Medium:	100 tablets for $7.80
Large:	150 tablets for $11.70

   What is the difference in dollars between the unit price of a tablet in the medium bottle and the unit price of a tablet in the large bottle? Please enter your response in the grid.

Test-Taking Tip

If you write a zero in a response grid, be sure to fill in the number 0 in the column below it. However, if you do not use a column in the grid, do not fill in the number 0. Leave the column completely blank.

6. Which ratios are the same as "7 to 2?"

   F $\frac{2}{7}$ and $\frac{7}{2}$

   G $\frac{2}{7}$ and 7:2

   H 7:2 and $\frac{7}{2}$

   J 2:7 and 7:2

7. A package containing 4 rolls of paper towels costs $6.36. A single roll of the same brand of paper towels costs $1.89.

Which statement is correct?

A It is more expensive to buy 3 single rolls than to buy the package of 4 rolls.

B You will save more than $1.25 if you buy the package of 4 rolls instead of 4 single rolls.

C If the cost of the package of 4 rolls is increased by $1.00, then the package will cost more than 4 single rolls.

D If the cost of a single roll is reduced by $0.30, then the cost of 4 single rolls will be equal to the cost of the package of 4 rolls.

Proportions

Proportions are used when changing the amount used in a recipe, reading maps, converting measurements, and in other applications.

Directions: Answer the questions below.

8. Megan earned $48 working 5 hours Friday afternoon. She plans to work 3 more hours Saturday morning. Consider this proportion Megan used to find the amount, t, she will earn Saturday if she is paid at the same rate.

$$\frac{t}{5} = \frac{48}{3}$$

What error did Megan make? How much will she actually earn on Saturday?

F She switched 3 and 5. She will earn $80.00 on Saturday.

G She switched 3 and 5. She will earn $28.80 on Saturday.

H She switched 48 and 5. She will earn $80.00 on Saturday.

J She switched 48 and 5. She will earn $28.80 on Saturday.

9. A company can make 500 screws in 4 seconds. What is the number of screws the company can make in 1 minute?

A 125

B 2,000

C 7,500

D 120,000

10. Two gallons of paint will cover 800 square feet, and you want to paint 1,800 square feet. How many gallons of paint do you need? Please enter your response in the grid.

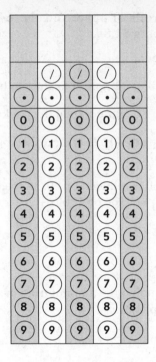

11. A 1.2-ounce bar of almond candy contains 240 calories. A 4-ounce bar of almond candy contains about how many more calories than the 1.2-ounce bar?

A 560

B 800

C 912

D 960

12. A bread recipe calls for 5 parts whole-wheat flour to 2 parts chickpea flour. You have $1\frac{1}{3}$ cups of chickpea flour and 4 cups of whole-wheat flour. If you bake the largest loaf possible using this flour, how many cups of whole-wheat flour will be left over? Please enter your response in the grid.

Scale

Scale drawings are used in many applications of architecture, engineering and maps because drawing buildings and maps with a 1:1 scale ratio is ineffective and impractical.

Directions: Answer the questions below.

13. To find the distance between two cities, Shawn looks at a state map. He measures the distance on the map between the cities to be $2\frac{1}{2}$ inches.

    Consider that the map scale reads 1 inch: 15 miles. What is the actual distance, in miles, between the cities? Please enter your response in the grid.

14. Jessica is 5.5 feet tall and casts an 8-foot shadow during the day. At the same time, a tree casts a 14-foot shadow. Assuming the ratio of height of an object to its shadow is proportional, what is the height of the tree rounded to the nearest thousandth of a foot?

    F 3.143

    G 9.625

    H 11.500

    J 20.364

15. The scale factor of a drawing of a building is 1 inch:48 feet. A drawing of the side of the building is 6.4 inches high. What is the actual height of the side of the building in feet?

    A 6.4

    B 41.6

    C 54.4

    D 307.2

16. Mike's regular pentagonal garden has sides measuring 8 feet. His neighbor builds a similar garden with a scale factor of $\frac{3}{2}$ to Mike's garden. What is the perimeter of his neighbor's garden in feet?

   F 20

   G 40

   H 60

   J 80

17. A wall in a new house has a height of 17 feet and a width of 19 feet. In a photo of the house, the width of the wall is 0.5 feet. What is the scale factor of the photo compared to the actual wall? Please enter your response in the grid.

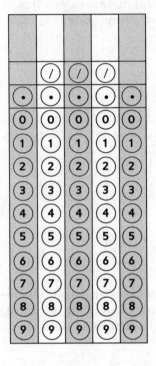

18. A building is 50 feet wide and 35 feet long. Which of these is the scale factor for the largest scale model of this building that can fit on a display base that is 20 inches wide and 20 inches long?

   F 4 inches:7 feet

   G 2 inches:5 feet

   H 7 inches:20 feet

   J 10 inches:7 feet

19. An isosceles triangle has a base of 6 inches. Each leg is triple the length of the base. A similar isosceles triangle has a base of 10 inches.

   Which of these is the length of one leg of the large triangle in inches?

   A 30

   B 54

   C 90

   D 108

This lesson will help you practice calculating percentages of a whole, percent change, and simple interest in real-world situations. Use it with Core Lesson 2.2 *Calculate Real-World Percentages* to reinforce and apply your knowledge.

Key Concept

A percent is a ratio of a number to 100. In fact, the word percent comes from the Latin term *per centum*, meaning "by the hundred," and it is represented by the symbol %. Fractions and decimals are also ratios, and they are related to percents.

Core Skills

- Use Tools Strategically
- Use Percent

Percent of a Number

Statistical information often appears as a percentage. The percent of a number describes a part of a whole, such as the part of a population that has a certain characteristic.

Directions: Answer the questions below.

1. A teacher records students' tests in her grade book as percentages. One student got 23 out of 25 correct. Which percentage should the teacher record?

   A 8%

   B 11%

   C 75%

   D 92%

2. A survey was taken by 300 runners, and 24% reported that they would rather run barefoot than wear a running shoe. How many runners surveyed prefer wearing a running shoe?

   F 24

   G 72

   H 228

   J 258

3. Out of 3,000 people surveyed at the beach, 79% of them answered "yes" when asked if they would go into the water above their waist. How many surveyed would go into the water above their waist?

   A 2

   B 24

   C 237

   D 2,370

Directions: Consider the information and table below to answer questions 4 and 5.

Susan's class made a table to show how many of them picked each color as their favorite.

Favorite Color	Number of Students
Pink	6
Red	4
Green	4
Blue	7
Purple	5
Black	2

4. **Susan said that 2.8% of students chose pink or red as their favorite color. Which statement is true?**

    F Susan is correct because she made the following calculation: $28 \div (4 + 6)$.

    G Susan is incorrect because she found $\dfrac{\text{total students}}{\text{students who chose pink + students who chose red}}$.

    H Susan is incorrect because she found $\dfrac{\text{students who chose pink}}{\text{total students}} + \dfrac{\text{students who chose red}}{\text{total students}}$.

    J Susan is correct because she found $\dfrac{\text{students who chose pink + students who chose red}}{\text{total students}}$ and then multiplied by 100.

5. **Which is not a correct way to calculate the percentage of students who chose pink or red as their favorite color?**

    A $\dfrac{4 + 6}{28} \times 100$

    B $(28 \div 10) \times 100$

    C $(10 \div 28) \times 100$

    D $\left(\dfrac{4}{28} + \dfrac{6}{28}\right) \times 100$

✅ Test-Taking Tip

Make sure to always use order of operations. Read left to right; first parentheses, then exponents, then multiplication or division, and finally addition or subtraction.

---

6. Consider this diagram.

The percentage of the diagram that is shaded can be written as a fraction with a denominator of 100. What is this fraction's numerator? Please enter your response in the grid.

Percent Change

A percent change is a way to compare the difference of an original amount to a new amount.

Directions: Answer the questions below.

7. The Outdoor Swimming Club offers a discounted membership if the membership is purchased during the winter. The fee is $126 when purchased during the winter and $180 when purchased during the spring or summer. What is the discount if a membership is purchased during the winter?

A −30%

B −54%

C 30%

D 70%

8. A clothing company originally priced a sweater at $54.99. They decided to discount the sweater by 20% during a sale. If each sweater cost $20.00 to manufacture, about how much profit will the company make if they sell 200 sweaters at the discounted price?

F $2,200.00

G $4,800.00

H $8,800.00

J $10,200.00

9. **Which item saves you the __most__ money?**

   A Original price $43.00; sales discount 5%

   B Original price $12.00; sales discount 30%

   C Original price $36.00; sales discount 15%

   D Original price $25.00; sales discount 20%

Directions: Use the information below to answer questions 10 and 11.

Ron is looking at prices of printers over the Internet. He finds a printer that was originally $212 and is now on sale for $159.

10. **Ron calculates the percent change in price to be 75%. Which statement best describes Ron's error?**

   F Ron divided 159 by 212 when he should have divided 212 by 159.

   G Ron correctly divided 159 by 212 but then he did not multiply by 100.

   H Ron divided 159 by 212 when he should have divided (212 − 159) by 212.

   J Ron correctly found the difference of 159 and 212 but then he did not divide by 212.

11. **Which of these is the correct discount?**

   A −25%

   B −75%

   C 25%

   D 75%

Directions: Answer the question below.

12. **A golf course offers a yearly membership. The first year it opened, the membership fee was $1,400. Consider the membership fees for the next five years.**

   Year 2: $1,200

   Year 3: $1,250

   Year 4: $1,500

   Year 5: $1,400

   Year 6: $1,450

   Which year had the greatest percent change from the previous year? Please enter your response in the grid.

Simple Interest

Simple interest can be money earned on an investment or money you owe for a loan.

Directions: Answer the questions below.

13. Eric has $2,000 to put into a savings account. Four banks have simple interest accounts from which Eric will choose. Which bank pays the most interest at the end of its term?

   A Bank A has a simple interest account that pays 3% per year for 4 years.

   B Bank B has a simple interest account that pays 2.5% per year for 5 years.

   C Bank C has a simple interest account that pays 4.2% per year for 3 years.

   D Bank D has a simple interest account that pays 1.75% per year for 8 years.

14. Suppose you deposit $10,000 into a bank account that earns simple interest at a rate of 2.99% per year. If you keep your money investment in the account and make no more deposits, how much will be in your account after 4½ years?

   F $1,196.00

   G $1,345.50

   H $11,196.00

   J $11,345.50

15. A student plans to borrow $20,000. Bank A charges a 4.2% simple interest rate per year for 10 years. Bank B charges a simple interest rate per year for 15 years. The student calculates that she will pay the same amount of interest for either loan. What is the simple interest rate at Bank B, as a percent? Please enter your response in the grid.

Directions: Consider the information and table below to answer questions 16 and 17.

Chad is buying a car for $5,000 from a used car dealership. The table below shows the total simple interest that will be paid for the first nine months.

Month	Total Interest Paid
March	$90
April	$180
May	$270
June	$360
July	$450
August	$540
September	$630
October	$720
November	$810

16. Which of these is the simple interest rate?

F 18% yearly

G 1.8% yearly

H 18% monthly

J 1.8% monthly

17. What is the total amount of interest paid, in dollars, for one year?

A $900

B $990

C $1,080

D $1,170

Directions: Answer the question below.

18. Kayla deposits $1,000 into a simple interest savings account on January 1st. She earns 5% simple interest per year. If Kayla does not deposit any more money into the account, how many years will it take for her to earn $1,000 in interest?

F 5

G 10

H 15

J 20

This lesson will help you practice understanding factorials and how to use combinations and permutations to count possibilities in probability situations. Use it with Core Lesson 2.3 *Use Counting Techniques* to reinforce and apply your knowledge.

Key Concept

Certain events can allow for uncertainty. When this occurs, it can be possible to determine the number of possible outcomes by using permutations and combinations.

Core Skills

- Use Counting Techniques
- Model with Mathematics

Factorials

Factorials show all the different ways a certain number of items can be arranged.

Directions: Answer the questions below.

1. **What does the number 5! equal? Please enter your response in the grid.**

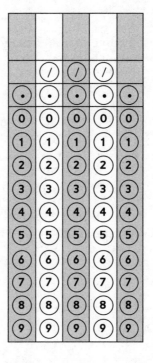

2. **Which number represents the total number of ways to order 6 people in a line?**

   F 21

   G 36

   H 120

   J 720

3. Jesse is trying to determine which of his three favorite rides to ride at an amusement park. He notices that there are 3 roller coasters, 3 merry-go-rounds, and 2 funhouses. What is the correct number of possible order choices for Jesse? Please enter your response in the grid.

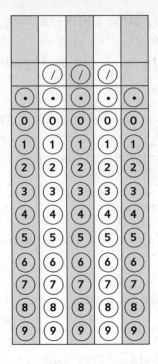

4. You flip a coin, select a card from a standard deck, and spin a 4-color spinner. How many different outcomes could there be?

F 58

G 104

H 208

J 416

5. What is the largest integer x such that $2^x > x!$? Please enter your response in the grid.

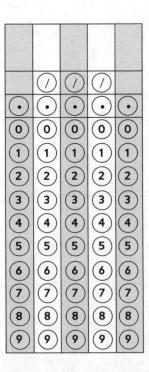

6. **The FunnyFace Kit advertises that you can make 1,000 different funny faces. Which kit <u>would not</u> live up to its advertising?**

    F   8 pairs of eyes, 7 pairs of ears, 4 noses, and 5 mouths

    G   3 pairs of eyes, 4 pairs of ears, 9 noses, and 6 mouths

    H   10 pairs of eyes, 3 pairs of ears, 7 noses, and 6 mouths

    J   2 pairs of eyes, 14 pairs of ears, 5 noses, and 8 mouths

7. **Anatole can choose from 105 different outfits. She has more tops than skirts, and more skirts than pairs of shoes. How many tops does she have? Please enter your response in the grid.**

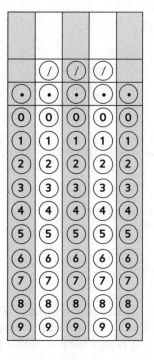

8. **Leon added an African violet to his collection of plants. Doing this added 600 different ways that Leon can line up his plants on his windowsill. How many plants does Leon have now? Please enter your response in the grid.**

Permutations

Permutations allow us to determine how many different ways a set of items can be ordered when order matters.

Directions: Answer the questions below.

9. **Which expression shows the number of permutations of 3 objects taken from 7 objects?**

   A $\dfrac{7!}{(7-3)!}$

   B $\dfrac{7!}{7!-3!}$

   C $\dfrac{7!}{3!(7-3)!}$

   D $\dfrac{7!}{3!(7!-3!)}$

10. **Lining up 5 different floats will allow how many different parades?**

    F 25

    G 120

    H 125

    J 3,025

11. **The PIN on your suitcase lock is three digits from 1 to 9 with none repeated, but you forgot the PIN. If you try one set of 3 digits every 5 seconds, what is the longest possible time, in minutes, it could take you to open the lock?**

    A 7

    B 42

    C 60

    D 83.25

12. **You are directing a historical play. How many ways can you cast the roles of Washington, Adams, and Jefferson from a pool of 8 actors?**

    F 24

    G 56

    H 336

    J 512

13. **How many different ways can Amos, Bill, Chuck, Debra, Esmeralda, and Florence be arranged for a photograph with the men on the left and the women on the right?**

    A 12

    B 36

    C 120

    D 720

14. **There are 380 ways the Springfield Begonia Society can elect a chairperson and a treasurer from among their members. How many members are in the society?**

    F 18

    G 19

    H 20

    J 21

15. **There are 210 ways to choose an opening act, a warm-up act, and a featured act for a comedy club. How many comedians are available?**

    A 5

    B 6

    C 7

    D 8

Combinations

Combinations allow us to calculate the number of possible ways to select a certain number of items when order doesn't matter, such as friends at a party.

Directions: Answer the questions below.

16. **Which of these cases involves finding combinations?**

    F Choosing the order in which to perform a set of 6 songs.

    G Choosing 3 out of a possible 7 toppings for a dish of ice cream.

    H Electing a president, a vice-president, and a secretary from 7 candidates.

    J Choosing first prize, second prize, and third prize from 25 photographs submitted in a contest.

✓ Test-Taking Tip

If you get confused when working with permutations and combinations, try drawing a tree diagram or making a chart. Then read the context of the question carefully to see if your answer makes sense.

17. Consider this table:

Toppings: mushroom, onion, anchovy	
1 topping	$6.95
2 toppings	$7.95
3 toppings	$8.95

What would be the cost to order all of the different pizzas that are available, assuming that each pizza must have at least one topping?

A $53.65

B $71.55

C $77.50

D $95.40

18. How many different floral bouquets can you make if each one contains 5 of 7 available flowers?

F 21

G 35

H 210

J 2,520

19. Keena wants to select 2 friends from a group of 5 to invite to dinner. "Now I have to sort through 20 possible combinations," she says. Is she right? If not, what is her mistake?

A No mistake; Keena is right.

B She should have found the factorial of 5.

C She should have used the Fundamental Counting Principle.

D She found the number of permutations instead of the number of combinations.

20. How many different ways can you award a first prize, a second prize, and two honorable mentions from among 8 contest entries?

F 70

G 840

H 1,680

J 3,360

This lesson will help you practice how to recognize and calculate real-world probabilities. Use it with Core Lesson 2.4 *Determine Probability* to reinforce and apply your knowledge.

Key Concept

The probability of a chance event uses a number between 0 and 1 to describe the likeliness that the event will occur. You can use the number of total and favorable outcomes of an event to determine the probabilities of simple or compound events.

Core Skills

• Determine Probabilities

Probability of Simple Events

We make decisions every day based on the likelihood of specific outcomes.

Directions: Answer the questions below.

1. Janine and her two children are attending Family Fun Night at the children's school. A drawing for a door prize will be held at 8:00 p.m. for all attending. If 390 people attend, what is the probability that someone in Janine's family will win the door prize?

   A $\frac{1}{390}$

   B $\frac{1}{130}$

   C $\frac{1}{13}$

   D $\frac{1}{3}$

2. A bag contains a red marble, a blue marble, a yellow marble, and a green marble. The probability of drawing a red marble is $\frac{1}{4}$. Which statement is correct in regard to the probability of drawing a blue, yellow, or green marble?

   F It is the supplement of drawing a red marble with a probability of $\frac{1}{4}$.

   G It is the supplement of drawing a red marble with a probability of $\frac{3}{4}$.

   H It is the complement of drawing a red marble with a probability of $\frac{1}{4}$.

   J It is the complement of drawing a red marble with a probability of $\frac{3}{4}$.

3. When rolling a number cube labeled 1–6, what is the probability of rolling an even number?

   A $\frac{1}{6}$

   B $\frac{1}{3}$

   C $\frac{1}{2}$

   D $\frac{2}{3}$

4. A company's uniforms consist of different colored shirts and pants. The shirts can be red, blue, or green. The pants can be tan or black. The tree diagram shows the possible color combinations. Which is the probability of randomly choosing a uniform that has a green shirt and black pants?

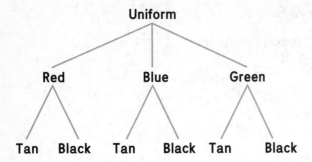

F $\frac{1}{9}$

G $\frac{1}{6}$

H $\frac{2}{9}$

J $\frac{4}{6}$

5. Elena thinks of a number from 1 to 50, and Sal tries to guess the number. Suppose Sal guesses the number 28. Which statement describes Sal's guess?

A Sal's guess is likely to be too low.

B Sal's guess is likely to be too high.

C The probability that Sal's guess is correct is $\frac{1}{28}$.

D The probability that Sal's guess is incorrect is $\frac{1}{50}$.

6. Consider this table.

Color of Cell Phone Covers	
Color	**Number**
Red	
Yellow	
Blue	8

This table shows the last 25 cell phone cover purchases at Cell Phone Hut. The best prediction for the number of red covers sold out of the next 100 sales is 40. What is the number that corresponds to the color red in the table? Please enter your response in the grid.

Probability of Compound Events

Often events happen in conjunction with other events, so the probability that an event occurs may sometimes depend on prior events.

Directions: Answer the following questions.

7. A spinner has 6 equal sections. Two sections are red, 3 sections are blue, and 1 section is green. What is the probability of spinning a red section twice?

    A $\frac{1}{9}$

    B $\frac{2}{6}$

    C $\frac{4}{6}$

    D $\frac{2}{3}$

8. A bag has 5 red marbles and 4 white marbles. Aaron draws a marble, sets it aside, and draws a second marble. What is the probability that Aaron will draw a white marble on both draws?

    F $\frac{1}{6}$

    G $\frac{3}{8}$

    H $\frac{4}{9}$

    J $\frac{5}{6}$

9. If you roll a number cube, labeled 1–6, thirty times, which outcome is most likely to occur?

    A Rolling a 5 thirty times

    B Rolling a 1, 2, or 3 three times

    C Rolling a 2 or 4 two times

    D Rolling a 3 five times

Test-Taking Tip

Make sure you understand the scenario of each question before choosing an answer. For instance, whether replacing or setting aside a card makes the second event independent, or dependent on the first event.

Directions: Consider these cards and coins to answer questions 10 and 11.

10. **Allen chooses one of the cards randomly and then flips the coin. What is the probability that Allen chooses a king and flips a head?**

    F $\frac{1}{8}$

    G $\frac{1}{4}$

    H $\frac{2}{6}$

    J $\frac{1}{2}$

11. **Emma chooses one of the cards randomly, sets it aside, and chooses a second card. What is the probability that Emma will choose a queen for both cards?**

    A $\frac{1}{2}$

    B $\frac{1}{3}$

    C $\frac{1}{6}$

    D $\frac{1}{12}$

12. **Consider this tree diagram.**

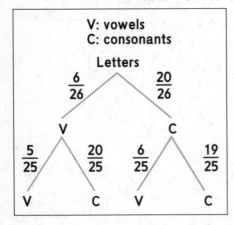

Peter has a bag of blocks. There is one block for each letter of the alphabet. The tree diagram shows the probabilities of drawing two blocks, without replacing the first block after it is drawn. What is the probability of drawing a vowel twice?

    F $\frac{3}{65}$

    G $\frac{12}{65}$

    H $\frac{6}{25}$

    J $\frac{20}{25}$

This lesson will help you practice using linear expressions to represent problems with one variable. Use it with Core Lesson 3.1 *Evaluate Linear Expressions* to reinforce and apply your knowledge.

Key Concept	Core Skills
There are a lot of unknowns around us. In math we do not always know the total we are solving for or the values we are calculating. These are expressions. Evaluating linear expressions means substituting values (numbers) for variables (letters).	• Perform Operations • Evaluate Expressions

Algebraic Expressions

An algebraic expression can be used to represent the cost of a product, the missing side of a polygon, or to find the height of an object at a specific time.

Directions: Answer the questions below.

1. A wedding hall charges $10 per person for food and $4 per person for beverages. The rental fee for the wedding hall is $350. If p represents the number of people attending, which expression represents the total cost for the wedding hall?

   A $350 + 10p - 4p$

   B $350 - 10p - 4p$

   C $350 + 10p + 4p$

   D $350 - 10p + 4p$

2. An airplane is at 35,000 feet when it starts to descend to the ground at the rate of 10 feet per second. If t represents the time in seconds, which expression represents the plane's descent?

   F $35,000 - 10t$

   G $35,000 + 10t$

   H $10t - 35,000$

   J $35,000 \times 10t$

3. The length of a rectangular garden is 4 times its width, minus 5. Which expression represents the perimeter of the garden if w represents the width of the garden?

   A $4w - 5 + w$

   B $2(4w - 5) + 2w$

   C $(2 \times 4w) - 5 + 2w$

   D $2(4w - 5) + w$

Test-Taking Tip

When reading a problem involving algebraic expressions, find key words in the problem. Words like plus, minus, decreasing, and increasing can help you determine the operation(s) needed to write the expression.

4. Robert works at a store during the holidays. He makes $12 per hour for a 40-hour work week and earns 1.5 times as much per hour for overtime. Which expression represents the amount Robert makes in a week if *h* represents the number of hours of overtime?

    F $12(40)$

    G $12(40) + 1.5h$

    H $12(40) + 12h$

    J $12(40) + 12(1.5)h$

5. A brand new truck costs $20,000. The truck depreciates in value by $3,000 as soon as it is driven off the lot. It also loses $175 per month in value after it is driven off the lot. What is the value of the truck after five years? Please enter your response in the grid.

6. Cole cuts a pizza into 12 equal slices. Cole takes *n* slices of the pizza and shares the remaining slices equally among 5 friends. Which expression tells the number of slices each friend gets?

    F $\dfrac{(n - 12)}{5}$

    G $\dfrac{(n - 5)}{12}$

    H $\dfrac{(12 - n)}{5}$

    J $\dfrac{(5 - n)}{12}$

Linear Expressions

A linear expression is a type of algebraic expression where terms have no more than one variable, and the variables do not have roots or exponents.

Directions: Answer the questions below.

7. Consider this algebraic expression.

$(7x - 8) + 2(x - 5)$

Which expression shows the correct simplification?

A $9x - 18$

B $9x - 3$

C $5x - 13$

D $5x - 18$

8. **Which expression would result from using distribution in the first step of the simplification of $(-3x + 10) - 4(x - 3)$?**

F $-3x + 10 - 4x - 12$

G $-7x - 2$

H $-3x + 10 - 4x + 12$

J $-7x - 7$

9. Consider this algebraic expression.

$2(x + 3) + 5(2x + 7)$

A student simplified this expression and her result was $12x + \underline{}$. What is the missing term of the simplified expression? Please enter your response in the grid.

10. Which of these expressions is the simplified form of the expression $-5(-3x + 2)$?

   F $15x - 10$

   G $-15x + 10$

   H $-15x + 2$

   J $15x + 2$

11. The expression $-2(-4x + 7) - 3(2x - 5) + a(2x + 6)$ is equivalent to $10x + 25$. What is the value of a in the first expression? Please enter your response in the grid.

12. Cassandra simplified the expression $(9y - 20) - (13y + 1)$ to $-4y - 19$. Which statement describes Cassandra's error?

   F She did not add the whole numbers correctly.

   G She did not combine like terms into one expression.

   H She did not multiply the 1 by -1 when distributing the coefficients.

   J She did not rearrange the expression so like terms are near each other.

13. Consider this expression.

$(4x - 17) + (-8x + 9) - 2(x - 14)$

How would the simplified form of the expression change if the coefficient of $(x - 14)$ was positive instead of negative?

   A It would be $-2x - 36$ instead of $-6x + 20$.

   B It would be $-4x - 54$ instead of $-14x - 2$.

   C It would be $-2x - 36$ instead of $-14x - 36$.

   D It would be $-4x - 20$ instead of $-10x + 54$.

Evaluating Linear Expressions

Linear expressions are evaluated when a value is substituted for the unknown.

Directions: Answer the questions below.

14. Consider this expression.

$$3 + \frac{3}{2}y$$

What is the value of the expression when $y = 2$?
Please enter your response in the grid.

15. Consider these expressions.

$$2x - 3y \qquad x - y \qquad 2x + y \qquad 3x + y$$

When $x = 5$ and $y = -3$, which expression has the greatest value?

A $2x - 3y$

B $x - y$

C $2x + y$

D $3x + y$

16. When $x = -2$ and $y = 4$, which expression has a value of 0?

F $3x + 2y$

G $2x + y$

H $4x + y$

J $5x + 2y$

17. The expression $18a + 7c$ can be used to find the total cost of going to the movies, where a is the number of adults and c is the number of children. What is the total cost for a group of 3 adults and 5 children to go to the movies?

A $8

B $25

C $89

D $111

18. An appliance company hires salespeople using different expressions to calculate their base pay and sales commission. The variable m represents the number of months, and s represents the monthly sales in dollars. Which person will earn the most after 6 months, assuming each salesperson sells $10,000 worth of appliances each month?

F Paula: $4,000m + 0.05s$

G Jakeem: $2,500m + 0.65s$

H Lorena: $3,500m + 0.45s$

J Michael: $1,500m + 0.85s$

19. Company A's cell phone plan charges a monthly fee of $25 plus $2 per GB of data used. Company B's cell phone plan charges a monthly fee of $20 plus $3 per GB of data used.

Which statement is true regarding the costs of using 3 GB of data in one month?

A Company A is a better deal.

B The plan under Company B is $2 more.

C The difference in cost between Company A and Company B is $2.

D The difference in cost between Company A and Company B is $4.

20. Three trash collection companies charge different rates. Take Your Trash charges $60 every 3 months, Dump Brothers charges $30 every month, while Garbage Removal charges $50 every 2 months.

Which statement is true regarding the costs of trash collection for one year?

F Take Your Trash is the most expensive.

G Dump Brother is $60 less per year than Garbage Removal.

H Take Your Trash company charges $180 for a one year period.

J The difference in cost between Garbage Removal and Dump Brothers is $60.

This lesson will help you solve one-step and multi-step equations. Use it with Core Lesson 3.2 *Solve Linear Equations* to reinforce and apply your knowledge.

Key Concept	Core Skills
You can solve an equation by performing inverse operations on both sides of the equation. The solution can be checked using substitution.	• Solve Simple Equations by Inspection • Solve Linear Equations

One-Step Equations

When solving equations, the goal is to find the unknown value.

Directions: Answer the questions below.

1. **Consider this statement.**

   A number tripled is 72.

   Write an equation to represent the statement and then solve your equation.

   A $n + 3 = 72; n = 69$

   B $3n = 72; n = 24$

   C $72n = 3; n = 24$

   D $n + 72 = 3; n = -69$

2. **Consider this statement.**

   Eight less than x is 31.

   Write an equation to represent the statement and then solve your equation.

   F $8 - x = 31; x = -23$

   G $8 + x = 31; x = 23$

   H $x + 8 = 31; x = 39$

   J $x - 8 = 31; x = 39$

3. **There are 150 people in a softball league. The sports director is going to divide all of the people into 10 equal teams. Write an equation that can be used to find the number of players, s, on each team and solve the equation.**

   A $150 \div s = 10; s = 15$

   B $150 \div 15 = s, s = 10$

   C $s \div 15 = 150, s = 10$

   D $15 \div s = 150, s = 15$

Test-Taking Tip

When writing equations from verbal descriptions, try substituting in values for your variable. If the answers you get do not make sense in the context of the problem, you may need to reevaluate the equation you wrote.

4. **On Thursday, a landscaper mowed 6 lawns. After paying $18 for gas, the landscaper had $90 left. Which equation can be used to find the amount of money the landscaper earned on Thursday?**

   F $90 = n + 18$

   G $90 = n - 18$

   H $90 = (n + 18) \div 6$

   J $90 = (n - 18) \div 6$

5. **Ginger sells copper pots for $45 each. How many copper pots did Ginger sell in one week if the cash register showed $1,800 at the end of the week? Please enter your response in the grid.**

6. **Which of these solutions is true for $-12h = 24$?**

   F 2

   G -2

   H $\frac{1}{2}$

   J $-\frac{1}{2}$

Multi-Step Equations

You can use multi-step equations for more complex calculations involving more than one operation.

Directions: Answer the questions below.

7. **Consider this statement.**

   5 plus the product of 4 and z is equal to 49.

   Write an equation and the solution to represent the statement.

   A $5z + 4 = 49; z = 9$

   B $z + 5 = 49; z = 44$

   C $4z + 5 = 49; z = 11$

   D $z + 4 = 49; z = 45$

8. **The amount of money b that Bob has saved and the amount of money j that Jody has saved are related by the equation $2b + 3 = j$. If Jody has saved $101, how much money has Bob saved?**

   F $49

   G $52

   H $202

   J $205

9. **If $8(m + 16) = 160$, what is the value of $9m$? Please enter your response in the grid.**

10. The difference of a number and 5 is multiplied by −9, and the result is 81. What is the number?

F −4

G 4

H −9

J 9

11. Keondre ate lunch at the same café 3 times during the past month. Each time, he ordered the same lunch and left a $2 tip. He spent a total of $39. What equation and solution represent the cost of each lunch <u>before</u> tipping?

A $3b - 6 = 39; b = \$15$

B $3b + 3 = 39; b = \$12$

C $3(b + 2) = 39; b = \$11$

D $3(b - 1) = 39; b = \$14$

12. What is the solution of $27 - 6x = -33$? Please enter your response in the grid.

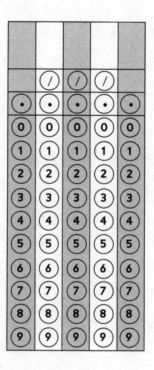

13. Which of these is the solution of $-18 = -3n + 30 - 9n$?

A −4

B 4

C −30

D 30

This lesson will help you practice representing real-world problems with linear inequalities, and solve algebraically or graphically on a number line. Use it with Core Lesson 3.3 *Solve Linear Inequalities* to reinforce and apply your knowledge.

Key Concept	Core Skills
Solving linear inequalities is very similar to solving linear equations, except the solution to a linear inequality will include a range of values, called the solution set. The solution set can be graphed on a number line.	• Represent Real-World Problems • Solve Inequalities

Inequalities

Inequalities are evident when there is a minimum value or a maximum value for an expression.

Directions: Answer the questions below.

1. **Which of these number line graphs represents the solution to the inequality** $x \leq -4$?

    A
    -4

    B
    -4

    C
    -4

    D
    -4

2. **An admissions officer accepts more than 312 boys in a high school. So far, 71 boys have been registered. If b is the remaining number of boys that need registered in the school, which inequality represents the situation?**

    F $b - 71 < 312$

    G $b - 71 > 312$

    H $b + 71 < 312$

    J $b + 71 > 312$

3. **Three times the sum of a number and 7 is greater than or equal to half of the number. Which inequality represents this situation?**

    A $3x + 7 \geq \frac{1}{2}x$

    B $3x + 7 > \frac{1}{2}x$

    C $3(x + 7) \geq \frac{1}{2}x$

    D $3(x + 7) > \frac{1}{2}x$

4. At a fundraiser, students sell items for \$8 per piece. The students must raise more than \$2,400 to buy new computers. Which inequality shows how many items the students must sell?

F ⊕ 300

G ◆ 300

H ◆ 300

J ⊕ 300

One-Step Inequalities

One-step inequalities require only one operation to find the solution set.

Directions: Answer the questions below.

5. Which of these is not a solution to the linear inequality $-3x < 8$?

A $x > -\frac{8}{3}$

B $x > -2\frac{2}{3}$

C $x > -2.666\ldots$

D $x > -\frac{3}{8}$

6. Which graph represents the solution to the inequality $x + 12 < 9$?

F ⊕ −3

G ⊕ −21

H ⊕ −21

J ⊕ −3

7. Which of these inequalities does not have -8 as a solution?

A $4x \geq -24$

B $\frac{x}{2} \leq -3$

C $x - 10 > -20$

D $x + 16 \leq 8$

8. Which graph represents the solution to the inequality $\frac{x}{-7} > 1$?

   F

   (number line with open circle near 8, shaded to the left)
   8

   G (number line with open circle at −7, shaded to the right)
   −7

   H (number line with open circle at −7, shaded to the left)
   −7

   J (number line with open circle near 8, shaded to the right)
   8

Test-Taking Tip

When solving inequalities, algebraically move the variable to the side of the inequality in which it will have a positive coefficient, or remember to always reverse the inequality sign if you have to multiply or divide by a negative number.

9. You need to make at least $1,000 profit from selling handmade jewelry. Your initial expenses were $400. Which graph represents how many dollars worth of jewelry you need to sell to meet your goal?

   A (number line with closed circle at 1400, shaded to the left)
   1400

   B (number line with closed circle at 600, shaded to the left)
   600

   C (number line with closed circle at 600, shaded to the right)
   600

   D (number line with closed circle at 1400, shaded to the right)
   1400

10. For a basketball team, Carden Jones has never scored more than 30% of the team's points during a game. He scored 21 points during the last game. Solve the inequality using p for the team's points to find the least amount of points the team could have made during the game. Please enter your response in the grid.

Multi-Step Inequalities

Multi-step inequalities have two or more operations and require more than one step to solve.

Directions: Answer the questions below.

11. You are ordering pizzas for your youth group with a total of $120 to spend. Each pizza costs $7.75 and you have a coupon for $10 off the total order. Using p to represent the number of pizzas, write and solve an inequality to find out the maximum number of pizzas that can be ordered. Please enter the solution to your inequality in the grid.

12. Solve and choose the correct graph of the inequality $3t - (5t + 10) > 4t + 2(t - 8)$.

F $\qquad \overset{\oplus}{\underset{\frac{3}{4}}{\qquad}}$

G $\qquad \overset{\bullet}{\underset{\frac{3}{4}}{\qquad}}$

H $\qquad \overset{\oplus}{\underset{\frac{3}{4}}{\qquad}}$

J $\qquad \overset{\bullet}{\underset{\frac{3}{4}}{\qquad}}$

13. Tom scored 91, 74, 83, and 86 on his first four math tests in class. He needs to have an average score of at least 85 to earn a B, and he has one more test to take. Which inequality and solution correctly represent the possible scores Tom can receive on the test to earn a B?

A $\dfrac{(91 + 74 + 83 + 86 + 85 + x)}{6} \geq 85; x \geq 91$

B $\dfrac{(91 + 74 + 83 + 86 + x)}{5} \geq 90; x \geq 116$

C $\dfrac{(91 + 74 + 83 + 86 + x)}{4} \geq 85; x \geq 6$

D $\dfrac{(91 + 74 + 83 + 86 + x)}{5} \geq 85; x \geq 91$

This lesson will help you practice using equations and inequalities to model real-world scenarios. Use it with Core Lesson 3.4 *Use Expressions, Equations, and Inequalities to Solve Real-World Problems* to reinforce and apply your knowledge.

Key Concept

Real-world problems can be translated into algebraic expressions, equations, and inequalities. Mathematical methods can then be used to find real-world solutions.

Core Skills

- Evaluate Expressions
- Solve Real-World Problems

Expressions and Equations

We use expressions and equations to model many real-world scenarios.

Directions: Answer the following questions.

1. Nick drives a taxicab. He charges a flat fee of $4 plus $0.25 per mile. How much does it cost, in dollars, to ride in Nick's taxicab for 8 miles? Please enter your response in the grid.

2. Freddy gets paid $25 for each lawn that he mows. He would like to buy a bicycle for $110 and has already saved $35. He wants to find the number of lawns he needs to mow to have enough money to buy the bicycle. Which equation models the situation?

   F $25n = 110 - 35$

   G $25n - 35 = 110$

   H $25n - 110 = 35$

   J $35n + 25 = 110$

3. On a recent trip, Hikari drove 165 miles. She stopped at a rest area for 15 minutes. The entire trip took 3.25 hours. Which equation can be used to determine the average speed (s, in miles per hour) that she drove during her trip?

   A $165 = s(3.25 - 15)$

   B $165 = s(3.25 - 0.25)$

   C $165 = 3.25s - 0.25$

   D $165 = 3.25 - 0.25s$

4. Which scenario matches the equation $150 - 8h = 54$?

   F Julie buys 8 lamps for a total of $150 and sells some for a profit of $54.

   G Julie has $150 to pay for cleaning services. She pays $8 for each hour of cleaning. She has $54 left afterwards.

   H Julie charges $150 for a cake and $8 for each hour she spends decorating it. She gives customers a $54 discount.

   J Julie has $54 to pay someone to paint her living room. She pays $8 for each hour of painting. She has $150 left afterwards.

5. Juan can run 1 mile in 12 minutes. Before running, he spends 5 minutes warming up. After running, he spends 10 minutes cooling down. Which expression models the total amount of time he spends running, including his warm-up and cool-down, if he runs m miles?

   A $5m + 12 + 10$

   B $12 + m(5 + 10)$

   C $5 + 1 + 12m + 10$

   D $5 + 12m + 10$

6. Bailey and Curt each borrow money from the bank. Bailey borrows $2,000 for 9 years. Curt borrows $2,700 at a 4% interest rate. Which shows the <u>rate</u> of Bailey's loan and the <u>length</u> of Curt's loan if they both have the same interest charges?

   F Bailey's rate: 3%, Curt's loan length: 5 years

   G Bailey's rate: 5%, Curt's loan length: 5 years

   H Bailey's rate: 2%, Curt's loan length: 2 years

   J Bailey's rate: 7%, Curt's loan length: 2 years

✓ Test-Taking Tip

When you enter your response on a grid on the test, make sure the characters you write match the characters you fill in on the grid and appear in the same row.

---

7. Marcella wants to buy a new treadmill. Today, the cost of the treadmill is $940 plus 6% sales tax. The store charges a $75 delivery fee at the end of the transaction. Starting next week, the treadmill will be on sale for 10% off. The sales tax and the delivery fee will remain the same. How many dollars will Marcella save if she purchases the treadmill next week and has it delivered to her home? Please enter your response in the grid.

8. Tyrell bought 4 pounds of apples and 3 pounds of pears at the grocery store. A pound of apples cost $2. Tyrell spent a total of $15.50 on the fruit. Which equation can be used to determine how much he paid per pound for the pears?

   F $4(2) + 15.50 = 3p$

   G $4p + 3(2) = 15.50$

   H $4(2) + 3p = 15.50$

   J $4p + 15.50 = 3(2)$

Inequalities

We use inequalities to model situations when expressions may or may not be equal.

Directions: Answer the following questions.

9. Edward has $1,000 to spend on new carpet in his house. Carpet costs $7 per square foot. How much carpet can he buy and still have $300 left for the installation fee?

    A no more than 100 square feet

    B no less than 100 square feet

    C more than 700 square feet

    D no less than 700 square feet

10. Hannah's car holds 16 gallons of gas. It can travel up to 32 miles on a gallon of gas. How many miles can Hannah drive on 1 tank of gas?

    F no more than 2 miles

    G fewer than 2 miles

    H fewer than 512 miles

    J no more than 512 miles

11. Miguel is preparing for a bicycle race and will train by riding at least 500 miles. So far he has ridden 360 miles on 18 different days. What is the smallest number of days that Miguel can ride at the same rate in order to meet his goal?

    A 5

    B 6

    C 7

    D 8

12. Consider this inequality.

    $5 - 2x \leq 35$

    A student solved the inequality and arrived at $x \leq -15$. Which statement best describes the student's work?

    F The student got the correct answer.

    G The student got the wrong answer because of incorrect division.

    H The student got the wrong answer because of incorrect use of inverse operations.

    J The student got the wrong answer because of forgetting to flip the inequality symbol.

13. Tara is planning a party. She has a budget of $60 for food and decorations. She plans to spend $15 on decorations. She also plans to buy pizzas that cost $8 each. Which inequality can be used to determine the number of pizzas that Tara will be able to buy?

A $60 - 8p \geq 15$

B $60 + 8p \leq 15$

C $60 < 8p + 15$

D $60 > 8p - 15$

14. Jake provides computer services. He charges a flat fee of $85 plus $30 per hour. Which inequality can be used to find the number of hours he needs to work on a project in order to earn at least $500?

F $30 + 85x > 500$

G $85 + 30x < 500$

H $85 + 30x \geq 500$

J $30 + 85x \leq 500$

15. An amusement park has a minimum height requirement of 54 inches to ride a roller coaster. Which inequality represents this situation, if h is used to represent a person's height in inches?

A $h < 54$

B $h > 54$

C $h \leq 54$

D $h \geq 54$

16. Jolene has $110 to spend on a night out. Which inequality can be used to represent how much she can spend, s?

F $s > 110$

G $s < 110$

H $s \leq 110$

J $s \geq 110$

17. Albert is given three earning options in his contract for a sales job. He can earn a fixed salary of $50,000. He also can choose a base salary of $32,000 a year plus 10% in commission on his total amount in sales or $25,000 plus 12% of his total amount of sales. Albert wants to earn more than $50,000 this year. Which amount of sales would be the least amount for the best option to be $32,000 a year plus 10% in commission, knowing that all options need to be more than $50,000?

A $180,000

B $200,000

C $225,000

D $300,000

18. Maddie has $450 in her bank account. She is going to visit her grandparents in California for 4 weeks and she must use her own money to pay for souvenirs and gifts while she is there. However, when she returns home she wants to have enough money left in her account to buy a new pair of boots that cost $230. How much money is Maddie able to spend at most each week and still be able to buy the boots? Please enter your response in the grid.

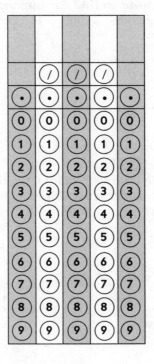

This lesson will help you practice evaluating polynomials and representing real-world problems with polynomials. Use it with Core Lesson 4.1 *Evaluate Polynomials* to reinforce and apply your knowledge.

Key Concept	Core Skills
Polynomials are special types of variable expressions with one or more terms. Each term has a variable raised to a whole number exponent or is a constant.	• Use Math Tools Appropriately • Evaluate Expressions

Identifying Polynomials

Polynomials are algebraic expressions that are a collection of constants, variables, and exponents.

Directions: Answer the questions below.

1. **Which expression is an example of a binomial?**

   A $-3x^2$

   B $5x^4 - 2x$

   C $x^3 - 7x + 10$

   D $x^6 - 4x^4 - 7x^2 + 1$

2. **What is the degree of the polynomial expression $2x^3 - 3x^2 + 5x - 8$? Please enter your response in the grid.**

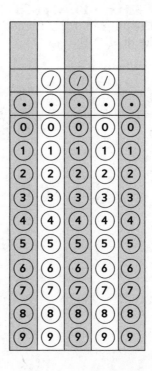

3. Which polynomial expression is **not** written in standard form?

   A $-6x^4 + 2x^3 - x + 5$

   B $-3x^2 - 2x + 4$

   C $x^2 - 6 + 7x$

   D $x^6 - x^4 + x^2$

4. Which statement does **not** describe a polynomial?

   F adding $-9x^2 + 7x$ to a constant

   G dividing a constant by $-9x^2 + 7x$

   H multiplying $-9x^2 + 7x$ by a constant

   J subtracting a constant from $-9x^2 + 7x$

5. Consider this polynomial expression.

$-6x^2 - 2x + 10 - 8 + 8x - 7x^2$

Which expression shows the polynomial above in simplified form?

   A $x^2 + 10x + 18$

   B $-13x^2 + 6x + 2$

   C $-x^2 + 6x + 2$

   D $13x^2 + 10x + 18$

6. If $(x - 2) \times B = x^3 - 5x^2 + 11x - 10$, where B is a polynomial, what is the degree of B? Please enter your response in the grid.

Evaluating Polynomials

In order to evaluate a polynomial expression for a given value, simply substitute the value into the variable in the expression and completely simplify the expression using order of operations.

Directions: Answer the questions below.

7. **Consider this polynomial expression.**

$-3x^2 - 5x + 10$

Miles evaluated this expression when $x = -2$. His work is shown below.

$$-3(-2)^2 - 5(-2) + 10$$
$$= -3(-4) - 5(-2) + 10$$
$$= 12 - (-10) + 10$$
$$= 12 + 10 + 10$$
$$= 32$$

Which statement is correct?

A Miles incorrectly evaluated the power.

B Miles correctly evaluated the expression.

C Miles made an error when subtracting a negative number.

D Miles made an error when multiplying two negative numbers.

8. **Consider this polynomial expression.**

$\frac{1}{2}x^3 + \frac{3}{4}x - 7$

What is the value of the expression when $x = 3$? Please enter your response in the grid.

✔ Test-Taking Tip

When evaluating a polynomial expression for a given value, substitute the value into the expression for the variable by first replacing the variable with a set of parentheses and then putting the value into the parentheses. Then, follow the order of operations to simplify the expression completely.

---

9. The height of a ball being thrown in the air can be modeled by the expression $-16t^2 + 38t + 5$, where t is the number of seconds since the ball was thrown. Which of these is the height of the ball, in feet, when $t = 2$ seconds?

A 17

B 49

C 93

D 145

Directions: Consider the rectangle below to answer questions 10 and 11. The dimensions shown are in feet.

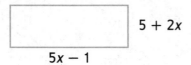

$5 + 2x$

$5x - 1$

10. If $x = 4$, what is the area, in square feet, of the rectangle?

F 64

G 123

H 247

J 532

11. Suppose the rectangle represents a region on a farm that is to be enclosed with a fence on all four sides. If $x = 20$, how many feet of fencing are necessary? Please enter your response in the grid.

Operations with Polynomials

When working with polynomials, it is often necessary to add, subtract, or multiply two or more polynomials.

Directions: Consider the rectangle below to answer questions 12 and 13. The dimensions shown are in feet.

$5 + 2x$

$5x - 1$

12. Which expression represents the area, in square feet, of the rectangle?

F $33x - 5$

G $7x^2 + 8x - 5$

H $10x^2 + 23x - 5$

J $10x^2 + 27x + 5$

13. Which expression represents the perimeter, in feet, of the rectangle?

A $7x + 4$

B $10x + 1$

C $14x + 8$

D $12x + 9$

Directions: Answer the questions below.

14. What is the product of $(x - 2)(2x^2 - x + 3)$?

F $2x^3 \; 6x^2 + x - 6$

G $2x^3 + 3x^2 + x - 6$

H $2x^3 - 5x^2 + x - 6$

J $2x^3 - 5x^2 + 5x - 6$

15. Consider this polynomial expression.

$(3x^3 + 4x^2 - x + 2) - (x^2 + 5x - 2)$

The first step in simplifying the expression is to find the opposite of the polynomial $x^2 + 5x - 2$. Which polynomial is the opposite of $x^2 + 5x - 2$?

A $x^2 + 5x - 2$

B $x^2 - 5x - 2$

C $-x^2 - 5x + 2$

D $x^2 - 5x - 2$

16. Consider this triangle that represents a portion of a pattern for a quilt. The dimensions shown are in centimeters.

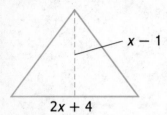

Which expression represents the amount of fabric, in square centimeters, needed to make 10 of these triangles?

F $x^2 - x - 2$

G $10x^2 + 10x - 20$

H $20x^2 - 20x - 40$

J $x^2 - x + 8$

17. Consider this rectangle that represents Justin's garden. The dimensions shown are in feet.

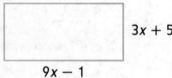

Justin wants to put a fence around his garden. Which polynomial expression represents the amount of fencing needed, in feet?

A $12x + 4$

B $24x + 8$

C $27x^2 + 42x - 5$

D $27x^2 - 48x - 5$

This lesson will help you practice solving problems involving real-world polynomials using various factoring methods. Use it with Core Lesson 4.2 *Factor Polynomials* to reinforce and apply your knowledge.

Key Concept	Core Skills
People practicing a variety of professions and hobbies write, simplify, and evaluate polynomial expressions. Polynomial expressions can be classified by their number of terms or by the greatest exponential power.	• Build Lines of Reasoning • Make Use of Structure

Factoring Out Monomials

To factor a polynomial means to write the polynomial as the product of two or more polynomials.

Directions: Use the trinomial shown to answer questions 1 and 2.

$$30x^4y^4 + 45x^2y^3 + 75xy^2$$

1. **Which of these monomials is the greatest common factor (GCF) of the trinomial shown?**

    A $5xy$

    B $5xy^2$

    C $15xy$

    D $15xy^2$

2. **Which of these is the factored form of the trinomial shown?**

    F $5xy(6x^3y^3 + 9xy^2 + 15y)$

    G $5xy^2(6x^3y^2 + 9xy + 15)$

    H $15xy(2x^3y^3 + 3xy^2 + 5y)$

    J $15xy^2(2x^3y^2 + 3xy + 5)$

Directions: Answer the questions below.

3. **What is the coefficient of the monomial $11xy^2$?**

    A 2

    B 11

    C x

    D y

4. What is the factored form of the binomial $9ab^2 + 18a^2b$?

   F $3(3ab^2 + 6a^2b)$

   G $9(ab^2 + 2a^2b)$

   H $3ab(3b + 6a)$

   J $9ab(b + 2a)$

5. What is the factored form of the expression $16x - 80$?

   A $2(8x - 40)$

   B $4(4x - 20)$

   C $16(x - 5)$

   D $16x(x - 5)$

6. Consider this trinomial.

$8mn^3 - 24m^2n - 12n^2$

What is the coefficient of the greatest common factor of the trinomial? Please enter your response in the grid.

7. What is the factored form of the trinomial $2xy^2 - 5y^2 - 10xy^3$?

   A $2xy(y - 5y - 5y^2)$

   B $2y^2(x - 5 - 5xy)$

   C $y(2xy - 5 - 10xy^2)$

   D $y^2(2x - 5 - 10xy)$

Factoring Quadratic Expressions

Oftentimes, real-world situations can be best modeled by quadratic equations and in order to solve quadratic equations, you must first know how to factor quadratic expressions.

Directions: Answer the questions below.

8. **What is the factored form of $x^2 - 8x + 7$?**

   F $(x + 7)(x + 1)$

   G $(x - 7)(x + 1)$

   H $(x - 7)(x - 1)$

   J $(x + 7)(x - 1)$

9. **Consider this quadratic expression.**

   $x^2 - ax - 24$, a is a positive integer

   What is the greatest possible value of a? Please enter your response in the grid.

10. **Which of these shows $4x^2 - 4x - 24$ factored completely?**

    F $(4x + 8)(x - 3)$

    G $4(x - 2)(x + 3)$

    H $4(x - 3)(x + 2)$

    J $4(x - 3)(x - 2)$

 Test-Taking Tip

Pay special attention to the positive and negative signs of numbers in factors, as this could help you quickly eliminate certain answer choices in a multiple-choice question.

11. Which of these shows $12x^3 + 2x^2 - 10x$ factored completely?

   A $(12x^2 - 10x)(x + 1)$

   B $(2x^2 + 2x)(6x - 5)$

   C $2x(6x + 5)(x - 1)$

   D $2x(6x - 5)(x + 1)$

12. What is the factored form of $6x^2 + 13x - 5$?

   F $(3x - 1)(2x + 5)$

   G $(3x + 1)(2x - 5)$

   H $(3x - 1)(2x - 5)$

   J $(3x + 1)(2x + 5)$

13. Which of these shows $8x^3 + 2x^2 - 3x$ factored completely?

   A $(2x^2 - x)(4x + 3)$

   B $(4x^2 - 3x)(2x - 1)$

   C $x(4x + 3)(2x - 1)$

   D $x(4x - 3)(2x + 1)$

14. Consider this trinomial that represents the area of a rectangle in square feet.

$A = (x^2 + 13x + 42) \text{ ft}^2$

The width of the rectangle is $(x + 6)$. What is the length of the rectangle?

   F $(x + 6)$

   G $(x + 7)$

   H $(x - 6)$

   J $(x - 7)$

15. A catapult is used to launch water balloons. The height of the balloon after t seconds, in feet, is given by the trinomial $(-16t^2 - 16t + 96)$. A student factored the trinomial and got $-16(t - 3)(t - 2)$. Which of these statements describes the student's work?

   A   The student's work is correct.

   B   The student's work is incorrect. The student did not factor out a GCF.

   C   The student's work is incorrect. The student factored out an incorrect GCF.

   D   The student's work is incorrect. The student factored out the correct GCF, but then incorrectly factored the trinomial.

This lesson will help you practice using equations and inequalities to model real-world scenarios. Use it with Core Lesson 4.3 *Solve Quadratic Equations* to reinforce and apply your knowledge.

Key Concept	Core Skills
Quadratic equations can be solved in several ways. Simple quadratic equations can be solved by inspection. More complex ones can be solved by factoring, completing the square, or using the quadratic formula.	• Reason Abstractly • Solve Real-World Problems

Solving a Quadratic Equation by Factoring

Factoring is one way to solve quadratic equations that can be used to describe the motion of an object or to calculate areas.

Directions: Use this information to answer questions 1 and 2.

The height of a baseball thrown during a game follows the curve shown in the graph after s seconds.

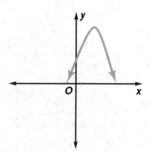

1. **Which of these is an appropriate value for the maximum height, in feet, for the ball?**

   A –5

   B 50

   C 250

   D 450

2. **If you are given the equation $y = x^2 + ax + b$ that models the path of the baseball and factor it as $y = (x - c)(x - d)$, which number describes how many seconds pass when the ball lands?**

   F $c - d$

   G $\dfrac{c + d}{2}$

   H the lesser value of c and d

   J the greater value of c and d

Directions: Answer the questions below.

3. Using the zero-product principle, what are the solutions to the equation $(x - 4)(x + 5) = 0$?

   A $x = 4$ or $x = 5$

   B $x = 4$ or $x = -5$

   C $x = -4$ or $x = 5$

   D $x = -4$ or $x = -5$

4. The product of two consecutive integers, x and $(x + 1)$, is 72. Which quadratic equation can be used to find the integers that satisfy the situation?

   F $(x^2 + 1) + 72 = 0$

   G $(x^2 + 1) - 72 = 0$

   H $x^2 + x - 72 = 0$

   J $x^2 + x + 72 = 0$

5. What is the sum of the solutions to the equation $x^2 - 23x + 132 = 0$? Please enter your response in the grid.

6. Consider this equation.

   $x^2 = 24 - 2x$

   What are the solutions to the equation?

   F $x^2 = -3, x = 8$

   G $x = -4, x = 6$

   H $x = 4, x = -6$

   J $x = 3, x = -8$

7. **How does the quadratic expression $6x^2 - x - 12$ factor?**

   A $(6x + 12)(x - 1)$

   B $(6x - 3)(x + 4)$

   C $(3x + 4)(2x - 3)$

   D $(3x - 3)(2x + 4)$

Completing the Square

Completing the square is another way to solve quadratic equations.

Directions: Answer the questions below.

8. **What is the value of c such that $x^2 + 14x + c$ is a perfect square trinomial?**

   F 7

   G 14

   H 28

   J 49

9. **Consider this work that Stanley used to solve the equation $x^2 + 4x - 2 = 0$ by completing the square.**

   Step 1: $(x^2 + 4x \quad) = 2$

   Step 2: $(x^2 + 4x + 4) = 2$

   Step 3: $(x + 2)^2 = 2$

   Step 4: $\sqrt{(x + 2)^2} = \pm\sqrt{2}$

   Stanley made an error. In which step did Stanley make an error?

   A Step 1

   B Step 2

   C Step 3

   D Step 4

10. **The distance d, in feet, that a dropped object falls in t seconds is given by the equation $d = 16t^2$. If a ball is dropped from the roof of a building that is 36 feet tall, how many seconds will it take to reach the ground?**

    F 0.5

    G 1.5

    H 4

    J 6

11. Consider these two equations.

$x^2 - 32x = -256$

$x^2 - 14x = 32$

What is the solution that the two equations have in common? Please enter your response in the grid.

12. Which equation has no real solution?

F $x^2 - 10x = -25$

G $-x^2 = -100$

H $x^2 - 25 = 0$

J $x^2 + 49 = 0$

13. Consider this equation.

$y = 3x^2 + 2x - 1$

What is the minimum value that the graph of the equation crosses the x-axis?

A -1

B $-\frac{1}{3}$

C $\frac{4}{3}$

D $\frac{1}{3}$

The Quadratic Formula

The quadratic formula allows you to solve any quadratic equation by substituting values into the formula.

Directions: Answer the questions below.

14. Consider this equation.

$3x^2 + 5x - 10 = 0$

How many real solutions does the equation have? Please enter your response in the grid.

Test-Taking Tip

When using the quadratic formula to solve a quadratic equation, the equation must first be written in the form $ax^2 + bx + c = 0$. The equation must also be written in the form $ax^2 + bx + c = 0$ when finding the discriminant.

---

15. Consider this equation.

$-4x^2 + 5x = 6$

To solve the equation using the quadratic formula, which values should be substituted for a, b, and c?

A $a = -4, b = 5, c = -6$

B $a = -4, b = 5, c = 6$

C $a = 4, b = -5, c = -6$

D $a = 4, b = 5, c = -6$

16. Consider this equation.

$$d = \frac{x^2}{20} + x$$

If you drive at x miles per hour and apply the brakes, your stopping distance, in feet, is approximately d. At what speed, in miles per hour, do you have a stopping distance of approximately 240 feet?

F 24

G 48

H 60

J 80

17. Consider this equation.

$$-4 + 2x^2 = 5x$$

Which expression shows the quadratic formula being applied correctly to the equation?

A $\dfrac{5 \pm \sqrt{25 - 4(2)(4)}}{2(2)}$

B $\dfrac{-5 \pm \sqrt{25 - 4(2)(-4)}}{2(2)}$

C $\dfrac{5 \pm \sqrt{10 - 4(2)(4)}}{2(2)}$

D $\dfrac{-5 \pm \sqrt{10 - 4(2)(-4)}}{2(2)}$

18. What are the solutions of the equation $3x^2 + 8x - 3 = 0$?

F $\dfrac{8 \pm 10}{4}$

G $\dfrac{-8 \pm 10}{4}$

H $\dfrac{-8 \pm \sqrt{28}}{6}$

J $\dfrac{-8 \pm 10}{6}$

19. An object is launched upward at a speed of 16 feet per second from a platform that is 5 feet high. The height, h, in feet, of the object after t seconds is given by the equation $h = -16t^2 + 16t + 5$. How long will it take, in seconds, before the object lands on the ground?

A 0.25

B 0.5

C 1

D 1.25

This lesson will help you practice adding, subtracting, multiplying, dividing, and evaluating rational expressions. Use it with Core Lesson 4.4 *Evaluate Rational Expressions* to reinforce and apply your knowledge.

Key Concept	Core Skills
A rational expression is a ratio of two polynomials. Rational expressions are similar to fractions and can be simplified, multiplied, divided, added, and subtracted using methods similar to those for fractions.	• Evaluate Expressions • Perform Operations

Simplifying Rational Expressions

This section will help you practice simplifying rational expressions, including finding restricted values for the original rational expression.

Directions: Answer the following questions.

1. **Which of these is a rational expression?**

   A $\dfrac{3}{2^x}$

   B $\dfrac{\sqrt{3}}{x}$

   C $\dfrac{3t^3 r^2}{r^{-2} s^4}$

   D $\dfrac{2p + 1}{\sqrt{p} - 2}$

2. **What is the restricted value of the rational expression $\dfrac{2x^2 + 3x - 2}{-x + 4}$? Please enter your response in the grid.**

3. **Which of these are the restricted values for the rational expression $\dfrac{2x}{x^3 - 9x}$?**

   A $-3, 3$

   B $-3, 0$

   C $-3, 0, 3$

   D 0

4. **Which shows the rational expression $\dfrac{x^3 - 4x}{x^2 - 4}$ correctly simplified with its restricted values?**

   F $x; x \neq -2, 2$

   G $x - 2; x \neq 4$

   H $x; x \neq -2, 0, 2$

   J $x + 2; x \neq 0$

✅ Test-Taking Tip

Cancelling factors in a rational expression can be thought of as dividing the denominator into the numerator. Since you can never divide by 0, you have to be careful to look for values where the cancelled factor would be 0 and list them as restricted values.

---

5. **Jack is taking a test on simplifying rational expressions.**

   Consider this test question:

   What is the simplest form of the rational expression $\dfrac{x^2 + 8x + 15}{x^2 - 9}$?

   Jack factors $\dfrac{(x + 5)\cancel{(x + 3)}}{(x - 3)\cancel{(x + 3)}}$. He is left with the rational expression $\dfrac{(x + 5)}{(x - 3)}$ as his final solution.

   Which statement correctly identifies his mistake?

   A Jack did not find the restricted value 9.

   B Jack did not find the restricted value -3.

   C Jack did not factor the numerator correctly.

   D Jack should have canceled $x + 3$ in the numerator and $x - 3$ in the denominator.

6. **Which expression is a simplified version of $\dfrac{(x - a)^{-3}(b - x)^2(x - c)^{-4}}{(x - a)^{-4}(b - x)^5(x - c)^{-2}}$?**

   F $\dfrac{(x - a)^{12}}{(b - x)^{10}(x - c)^3}$

   G $\dfrac{(x - a)^{-1}}{(b - x)^{-3}(x - c)^{-2}}$

   H $\dfrac{(x - a)^7}{(b - x)^7(x - c)^6}$

   J $\dfrac{(x - a)}{(b - x)^3(x - c)^2}$

Multiplying and Dividing Rational Expressions

This section will help you practice multiplying and dividing rational expressions.

Directions: Answer the following questions.

7. **Which of these should you do first when multiplying rational expressions?**

   A Find the LCD.

   B Add the denominators.

   C Factor each rational expression and simplify.

   D Rewrite the expression as multiplication by the reciprocal.

8. **Consider this operation on rational expressions.**

   $$\frac{x^2 + 2x - 8}{2x^2 + 8x} \cdot \frac{x^2 + x - 12}{x^2 - 3x}$$

   What is the rational expression simplified and the restricted values?

   F $\dfrac{x^2 + 2x - 8}{2x^2}; x \neq -4, 0, 3$

   G $\dfrac{x^2 + x - 12}{2x^2}; x \neq -4, 3$

   H $\dfrac{x^4 + 3x^3 - 18x^2 - 32x + 96}{2x^4 + 2x^3 - 24x^2}; x \neq \sqrt{3}, -\sqrt{3}, 2, -2$

   J $\dfrac{32x + 82}{-20}; x \neq -4, 0, \sqrt{3}, 2$

9. **Consider this simplification of the rational expression.**

   $$\frac{x^3 + x^2 - 9x - 9}{x^2 + x - 12} \div \frac{x^2 + 4x + 3}{x^2 - 4} = \frac{x^2 + ax - 4}{x + 4}; x \neq -1, -3, 3$$

   What is the value of a? Please enter your response in the grid.

10. Find the area of the rectangle shown.

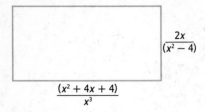

$$\frac{2x}{(x^2 - 4)}$$

$$\frac{(x^2 + 4x + 4)}{x^3}$$

F $\dfrac{-2}{x^2}$

G $\dfrac{2x + 4}{x^3 - 2x^2}$

H $\dfrac{-2}{x^2 + 2}$

J $\dfrac{2x - 2}{x^3 + 2}$

11. Consider the procedure for multiplying fractions and the procedure for multiplying rational expressions. Which statement <u>incorrectly</u> analyzes the similarities or differences between these two procedures?

A Both procedures can simplify before multiplying.

B A difference is that rational expressions have restricted values.

C Both procedures find the sum of the numerators and the product of the denominators.

D A difference between multiplying fractions and rational expressions is that the solution can vary for the rational expression. There is only one value for a fraction because it is a constant.

12. The volume of water in a rectangular pool can be written as $\dfrac{(x + 4)(x - 1)}{x(x + 2)}$ cubic units. The length and width of the pool are $\dfrac{(x + 4)^2(x - 1)}{(x + 1)(x - 2)}$ units and $\dfrac{(x - 2)^2(x + 1)}{x^2(x + 4)(x - 3)}$ units, respectively. What is the height of the pool?

F $\dfrac{(x + 4)(x + 2)}{x(x - 3)}$

G $\dfrac{x(x - 3)}{(x - 2)(x + 2)}$

H $\dfrac{(x + 1)^2(x - 3)}{x^2(x - 2)}$

J $\dfrac{(x - 1)(x + 2)}{x(x - 4)}$

Adding and Subtracting Rational Expressions

In this section you will get practice adding and subtracting rational expressions in a real-world scenario.

Directions: Use this information to answer questions 13 and 14.

The boat called the Rapids starts at port Seeyalateralligator and moves down the river with the current towards port Inawhilecrocodile. The boat called the Bayou starts at port Inawhilecrocodile and heads up the river against the current towards the port Seeyalateralligator. The Rapids takes x hours to travel from Seeyalateralligator to Inawhilecrocodile, and the Bayou travels half as fast due to the current.

13. **What fraction of the total distance between Seeyalateralligator and Inawhilecrocodile have the Rapids and the Bayou travelled together in an hour?**

    A $\frac{3}{x}$

    B $\frac{3}{2x}$

    C $\frac{x}{3}$

    D $\frac{2x}{3}$

14. **If it takes the Rapids 2 hours to complete the trip, then rounded to the nearest tenth how many hours will it take them to cross each other's path? Please enter your response in the grid.**

Directions: Use this information to answer questions 15 and 16.

Susan has to paint the bottom of two rectangular swimming pools. The volume of the first pool is $x^3 + 12x^2 + 20x$ with a depth of $x + 2$. The volume of the second pool is $2x^3 + 7x^2 + 3x$ with a depth of $2x + 1$.

15. What is the total area that needs to be painted for the two pools?

A $7x$

B $2x^2 + 13x$

C $\dfrac{2x + 13}{x^3 + 13x^2 + 30x}$

D $\dfrac{7}{x^3 + 13x^2 + 30x}$

16. Which statement is <u>incorrect</u>?

F The restricted values are irrelevant.

G When $x = \frac{1}{2}$, the square units are not defined.

H When $x = 1$, 15 square units of paint are needed.

J The area of the bottom of the first pool is larger than the area of the bottom of the second pool.

Directions: Answer the following question.

17. Rita can build a house in $x + 7$ weeks. Jarod can build the same house in $x + 2$ weeks. Sean can build the house in $x - 1$ weeks. Emma can build the house in $x + 12$ weeks. Which statement is <u>not</u> true?

A There are no restricted values for x.

B If $x = 3$, it will take all four of them $1\frac{2}{13}$ weeks to build a house.

C Rita and Jarod will get $\dfrac{2x + 9}{x^2 + 9x + 14}$ of the house built in one hour.

D Sean and Emma will get $\dfrac{2x + 11}{x^2 + 11x - 12}$ of the house built in one hour.

This lesson will help you practice analyzing slope or rate of change in real-world scenarios. Use it with Core Lesson 5.1 *Interpret Slope* to reinforce and apply your knowledge.

Key Concept

Slope, a measure of the steepness of a line, is the ratio of vertical change to horizontal change (or rise over run). For lines that represent proportional relationships, the slope of the line is equal to the unit rate.

Core Skills

- Make Use of Structure
- Use Ratio Reasoning

Points and Lines in the Coordinate Plane

The coordinate plane is a convenient way to plot points from an equation or table.

Directions: Answer the questions below.

1. **Which statement is correct?**

   A The point $(-3, -6)$ is in Quadrant I.

   B The point $(-2, 1)$ is in Quadrant II.

   C The point $(1, -1)$ is in Quadrant III.

   D The point $(2, 3)$ is in Quadrant IV.

2. **Look at this graph.**

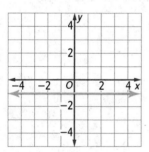

   Which of these ordered pairs is a solution to the equation of the line in the graph?

   F $(-3, 2)$

   G $(-1, 2)$

   H $(4, -1)$

   J $(-2, -3)$

3. **Which of these groups of points are on the line $y = -x$?**

A $(-2, -1), (0, 0), (2, 1)$

B $(-2, 1), (0, 0), (2, -1)$

C $(-2, 2), (0, 0), (2, -2)$

D $(-2, -2), (0, 0), (2, 2)$

4. **Which of these table of values represents $y = -x + 2$?**

F

x	y
1	3
2	4
3	5

G

x	y
0	2
1	3
2	4

H

x	y
−2	0
−1	−1
0	−2

J

x	y
−1	3
0	2
1	1

The Slope of a Line

The slope of a line can describe speed, pay rates, interest rates, or the cost of items.

Directions: Answer the questions below.

5. **Which of these graphs has a slope of $\frac{1}{2}$ and crosses the y-axis at a negative value?**

A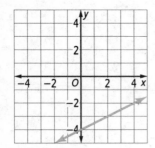

B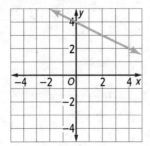

C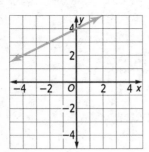

D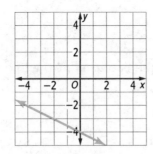

6. Consider this table. It represents a linear relationship.

x	y
−2	−4
−1	−2
0	0
1	2

Helen used the slope formula and said that the slope of this line is −2. Her calculations are shown below.

$$\frac{(-4 + 2)}{(-1 + 2)} = -2$$

Which of these errors did Helen make? What is the correct slope?

F Helen did not make an error. The correct slope is −2.

G Helen used addition instead of subtraction. The correct slope is 2.

H Helen did not subtract coordinates in the same order in the numerator and the denominator. The correct slope is 2.

J Helen substituted x-coordinates in the numerator and y-coordinates in the denominator. The correct slope is $-\frac{1}{2}$.

 Test-Taking Tip

For multiple-choice questions, one strategy is to first eliminate the answers you know are incorrect and then proceed forward.

---

7. Which of these graphs has a slope of 0.75?

A
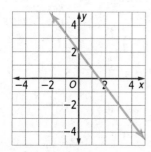

B
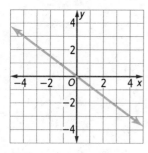

C
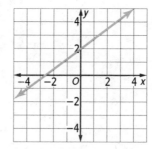

D
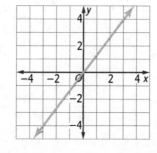

8. **For a line that has a positive slope, how do the values of y change from left to right?**

    F The values of y increase from left to right.

    G The values of y decrease from left to right.

    H The values of y do not change from left to right.

    J The values of y first increase and then decrease from left to right.

9. **A track coach timed her athletes as they ran. She described each student's run as an ordered pair where x represents minutes and y represents distance run in miles. She noticed that three of the ordered pairs formed a line. The three ordered pairs were:**

    (6, 1)

    (13, 2)

    (20, 3)

    What is the slope of the line through these points? Please enter your response in the grid.

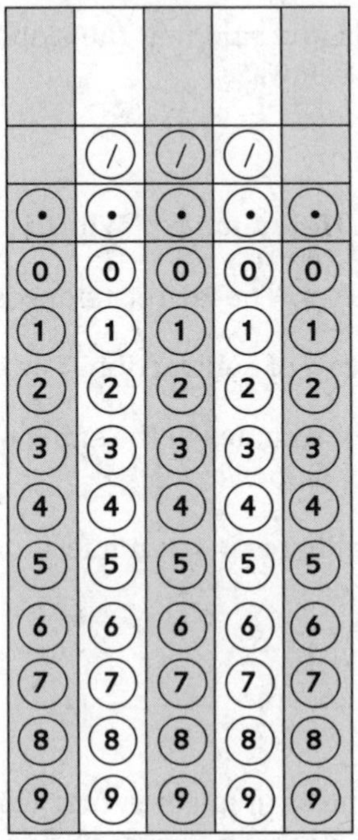

10. **A set of ordered pairs is shown below. What is the slope of the line that contains these points?**

    (0, 0)   (6.5, 1)   (13, 2)   (19.5, 3)

    F 0

    G $\dfrac{2}{39}$

    H $\dfrac{1}{13}$

    J $\dfrac{2}{13}$

Slope as a Unit Rate

Knowing the slope in a real-world proportional relationship helps you better understand the relationship between the variables.

Directions: Answer the questions below.

11. Consider these graphs that represent the cost, y, to download x music albums from different Web sites.

Web site A

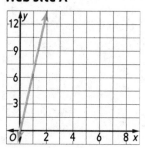

Web site B

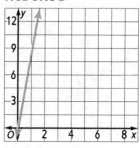

Web site C

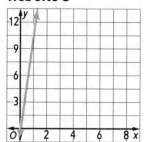

Web site D

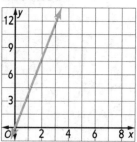

Which of these Web sites charges the most to download an album?

A Web site A

B Web site B

C Web site C

D Web site D

12. Consider this graph and equation that describe the cost, y, of hiring two different painters for x hours.

Painter A

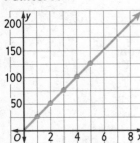

Painter B

$y = 35x$

Which statement is false?

F Painter A charges by the hour.

G Painter A is less expensive than Painter B.

H Painter A charges $5.00 less per hour than Painter B.

J Painter B charges $10.00 more an hour than Painter A.

13. Two rowers each traveled at a constant rate of speed. Consider the table and equation that describe the distance in miles, y, traveled by each rower in x hours.

Rower A

$y = 10x$

Rower B

Hours, x	Miles, y
1	15
2	30
3	45

What is the difference in miles traveled between the two rowers after 2.5 hours? Please enter your response in the grid.

14. Consider this table that shows data about the number of words texted, y, in x minutes.

Time in minutes, x	Words texted, y
3	150
6	300
9	450

Which of these is the unit rate in words per minute?

F 1

G 3

H 50

J 150

15. Consider this graph.

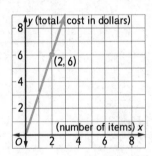

Which of these is the best description of the unit rate shown in the graph?

A $3.00 per item

B $1.00 per 3 items

C 6 items per $2.00

D 0 items per $0.00

16. Consider these graphs.

Graph A

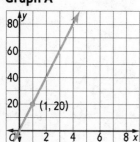

Graph B

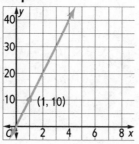

Ken said that these lines have the same slope, so the unit rates are equal. Which statement best describes why Ken is incorrect?

F   Slope and unit rate are not related.

G   Two different lines cannot have the same slope.

H   The lines have the same slope, but the unit rates are different because the lines pass through different points.

J   The lines appear to have the same slope but the scales on the y-axes are different, and therefore the slopes and unit rates are different.

17. Consider the table and graph below that show the cost in dollars, y, of purchasing x printer cartridges at two different stores.

Store A

Number of Cartridges, x	Cost, y
4	$50.00
8	$100.00
12	$150.00

Store B

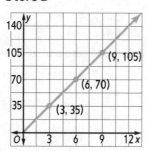

What is the difference in the prices, in dollars, of purchasing one printer cartridge? Please enter your response in the grid.

This lesson will help you practice writing the equation of a line from points, slopes, tables, graphs, or real-world scenarios. Use it with Core Lesson 5.2 *Write the Equation of a Line* to reinforce and apply your knowledge.

Key Concept	Core Skills
The equation of a line can be written in many different ways. You can use given information about the line to determine the best way to write the equation.	• Build Solution Pathways • Model with Mathematics

Using Slope and y-Intercept

You can use the slope-intercept form to express real-life scenarios that have a membership fee and the same cost per item or service.

Directions: Answer the questions below.

1. **Consider this equation.**

   $y = 0.25x - 5$

   A student said that the standard form of this equation is $0.25x - y = 5$. Which statement describes why this student is incorrect?

   A The coefficient of y may not be negative.

   B The right side of the equation should be -5.

   C The coefficient of x must be a whole number.

   D The student has written the equation in slope-intercept form.

2. **Which equation represents the line with a positive slope and a negative y-intercept?**

   F $3x + y = 2$

   G $y - 2 = 3x$

   H $y = 3x + 2$

   J $y = 3x - 2$

3. **Which equation represents the line that contains the point (2, 4) and has a slope of 3?**

   A $y = 3x$

   B $y = 3x - 2$

   C $y - 3 = 4(x - 2)$

   D $y - 2 = 3(x - 4)$

4. On an online video rental site, there is a one-time membership fee and a cost of $1.00 to rent each video. The total cost to rent 3 videos is $8.00. Which equation can be used to find the cost, y, of renting x videos?

F $y = x$

G $y = 3x$

H $y = 11$

J $y = x + 5$

5. At a food co-op, there is a one-time membership fee of $8.00. Members can buy bulk food for $4.00 per pound. Which equation describes the relationship between the number of pounds of food purchased, x, and the total cost, y?

A $y = 4x + 8$

B $y = 8x + 4$

C $4x + 8y = 0$

D $8x + 4y = 0$

6. A line has a slope of 4 and contains the point $(-2, 1)$. What is the y-intercept? Please enter your response in the grid.

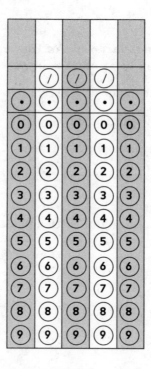

7. A line has slope $-\frac{1}{2}$ and contains the point $(-3, -2)$. Which of these is the equation of this line in point-slope form?

A $y = -2x - 2$

B $y = -\frac{1}{2}x - \frac{1}{2}$

C $y + 2 = -\frac{1}{2}(x + 3)$

D $y + 2 = -2(x + 3)$

Test-Taking Tip

Take care to note if a question asks for an answer in a particular format. Mathematical quantities and relationships can often be written in equivalent forms, but questions may require you to find one particular form.

8. The equation of a line is $y - 7 = \frac{1}{5}(x - 3)$. Which of these shows the slope of this line and a point on the line?

    F   Slope: 5; point: $(3, 7)$

    G   Slope: $\frac{1}{5}$; point: $(3, 7)$

    H   Slope: 5; point: $(-3, -7)$

    J   Slope: $\frac{1}{5}$; point: $(-7, -3)$

Using Two Distinct Points

Knowing just two data points for a linear relationship allows you to write the equation of the line.

Directions: Answer the questions below.

9. **Consider this graph.**

    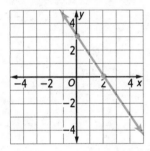

    Which of these is the equation in standard form of the line in the graph?

    A $2x - 3y = 6$

    B $3x - 2y = 6$

    C $3x + 2y = 6$

    D $2x + 3y = 6$

10. A line contains the points $(-2, 4)$ and $(-1, 2)$. Which of these is the equation of this line in slope-intercept form?

    F $y = 2x$

    G $y = -2x$

    H $y = -2x + 8$

    J $y - 2 = 2(x + 1)$

11. One day, Sophie parked in a parking garage for 2 hours. Her total fee was $18.00. The next day, Sophie parked in the same garage for 4 hours, and her total fee was $26.00. How much will it cost Sophie, in dollars, to park in the garage for 7 hours? Please enter your response in the grid.

Using Tables

Tables are a convenient way to record data to be converted to a graph.

Directions: Answer the questions below.

12. The table below gives the total earnings for a person whose monthly salary is $2,550 and who receives a bonus of $5,000 at the beginning of the year.

x Months Worked	y Total Earnings for the Year
0	$5,000
1	$7,550
2	$10,100
3	$12,650

Which statement is true?

F The point (0, 0) is on the graph of this relationship.

G The equation $y = 2,550x - 5,000$ describes the relationship.

H The total earnings for month 4 can be found by adding $2,550 to $12,650.

J If this person does not work for a month, his or her total earnings will decrease.

13. Carly decided to save her weekly allowance. The table below gives data for the total amount of money Carly saved after *x* weeks.

x Weeks	y Total Money Saved
0	$7.00
1	$16.00
2	$25.00
3	$34.00
4	$43.00
5	$52.00

Which statement is incorrect?

A Carly's weekly allowance is $9.00.

B Carly had $7.00 when she started saving.

C A graph of Carly's savings will be a line.

D After 8 weeks, Carly will have saved more than $80.00.

14. Consider this graph.

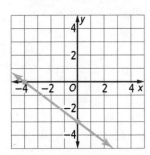

Which table describes the line in the graph?

F

x	y
−4	0
0	−3
4	−6

G

x	y
−4	0
−3	0
4	3

H

x	y
−4	0
0	−3
3	−6

J

x	y
−3	−4
3	−3
4	−6

15. Consider this table representing a linear relationship.

x	1	2	3	4	5	6
y	6	9	12	15	18	21

Which of these is the slope-intercept form of the equation that describes the table?

A $y = 3x$

B $y = -3x$

C $y = 3x - 3$

D $y = 3x + 3$

16. Consider this table that gives the coordinates of several points on a line.

x	y
−8	−3
−4	−2
0	−1
	1

What is the missing x-value? Please enter your response in the grid.

17. Consider this table representing a linear relationship.

x	1	2	3	4	5	6
y	1	2	3	4	5	6

Which of these real-world scenarios would the table not represent?

A Each item costs $1.00.

B Bob runs 1 mile every 10 minutes.

C Each hanger has 1 piece of clothing on it.

D Ruth earns 1 hour of TV time for every chore completed.

This lesson will help you practice graphing real-world problems involving linear relationships. Use it with Core Lesson 5.3 *Graph Linear Equations* to reinforce and apply your knowledge.

Key Concept	Core Skills
You can visualize how two variables in an equation are related by graphing the equation. Solutions of a linear equation can be plotted as ordered pairs on the coordinate plane. You can also use the special forms of linear equations to graph them.	• Solve Linear Equations • Interpret Graphs

Using Ordered Pairs

The graph of specific ordered pairs that shows a linear relationship between two measurable variables is helpful in finding other ordered pairs that have the same relationship.

Directions: Answer the questions below.

1. **Which table shows values from the equation $12x - y = 4$?**

A

x	y
0	−4
1	−8
2	−20

B

x	y
0	−4
1	8
2	20

C

x	y
0	4
1	8
2	20

D

x	y
0	4
1	−8
2	−20

2. **Consider the linear equation $y = 2x$.**

   Which ordered pair would <u>not</u> be in the table of values for this equation?

   F (1, 1)

   G (0, 0)

   H (1, 2)

   J (2, 4)

3. Consider this table.

x	y
0	1
1	4
2	7

Which graph represents the table?

A
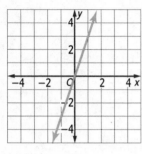

B
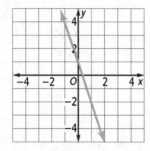

C
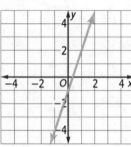

D
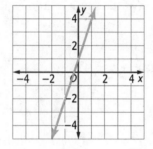

4. Consider this table that has partial ordered pairs for the equation $y = -2x - 3$.

x	y
−4	
	−11

What are the missing values? Leave an empty column between the missing y-value and x-value. Please enter your response in the grid.

5. Consider this graph of a linear equation.

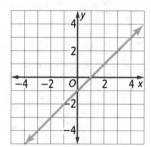

Which ordered pair would not be on this graph?

A $(0, -1)$

B $(1, 0)$

C $(2, 1)$

D $(3, 4)$

Directions: Use the information below to answer questions 6 and 7.

Mike ran 8 miles in 60 minutes at a steady pace. He wants to make a graph of his run that shows how far he ran every 15 minutes.

6. Which graph accurately represents Mike's run and displays the data he wants?

F

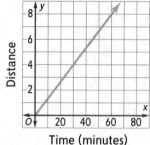

Time (minutes)

G

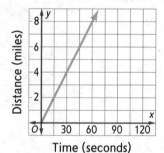

Time (seconds)

H

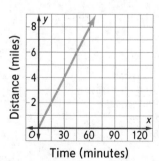

Time (minutes)

J

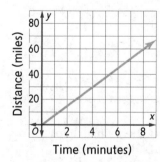

Time (minutes)

7. Which of these points is __not__ on the correct graph for Mike's situation?

A $(90, 12)$

B $(150, 20)$

C $(120, 12)$

D $(105, 14)$

Using Slope-Intercept Form

The slope-intercept form of a linear equation is an efficient way to graph a line versus plotting points to graph the line.

Directions: Answer the questions below.

8. **Which scenario could be represented by a line?**

    F   How many albums, y, you have of each artist, x.

    G   How many albums, y, you download each month, x.

    H   How much you spent, y, throughout the year on music items, x.

    J   The total cost, y, of downloading x number of albums at $2 per album.

9. **What is the slope of the graph chosen from below that has negative slope but positive y-intercept? Please enter your response in the grid.**

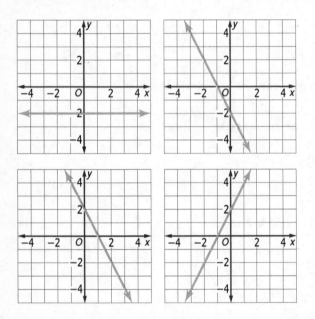

10. **Consider Harold's graph of the equation $y = -2x + 2$.**

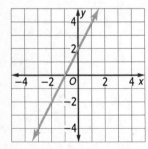

    He began by plotting the y-intercept. He then moved 2 units down and 1 unit to the left and plotted point $(-1, 0)$. What mistake did he make in his steps to graph $y = -2x + 2$?

    F   He plotted the incorrect y-intercept.

    G   His last step of plotting the point $(-1, 0)$ was wrong.

    H   Starting at the y-intercept, he then moved 2 units down.

    J   After moving 2 units down, he moved 1 unit to the left.

11. **Gina can type a text message at a rate of 100 words per minute. Her friend can type a text at 90 words per minute. If they make a linear graph for each of their rates, which statement would not be true?**

   A They would both have the same y-intercept.

   B They would both have the same x-intercept.

   C Their graphs intersect at more than one point.

   D Gina's slope would be greater than her friend's slope.

Directions: Consider these graphs and information to answer questions 12 and 13.

Graph A

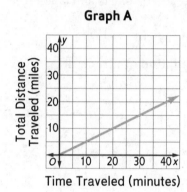

Time Traveled (minutes)

Graph B

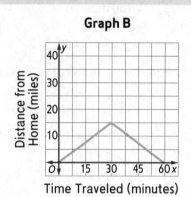

Time Traveled (minutes)

Both graphs represent the scenario of driving to work and back again at a constant speed of 30 miles per hour.

12. **Which statement is false?**

   F Work is 15 miles from the house.

   G Total distance traveled was 30 miles.

   H Graph A: After driving for 40 minutes, you are 20 miles from home.

   J Graph B: After driving for 40 minutes, you are 10 miles from home.

13. **Which equation represents the graph for Distance from Home when $x \geq 30$.**

   A $y = 15x + 30$

   B $y = -\frac{1}{2}x + 60$

   C $y = \frac{1}{2}x$

   D $y = -\frac{1}{2}x + 30$

✔ Test-Taking Tip

When graphing, make sure that you are aware of the scale on each axis so that the points you draw are accurate to that scale. This awareness also ensures that you are reading and interpreting a graph correctly.

Directions: Answer the questions below.

14. Choose the scenario that has a graph with a decreasing slope.

F Kate runs 6 miles per hour. She records the number of miles y she runs in x minutes.

G A company sells an item for $12.00. Let x be the number of items sold and y be the total sales.

H Brian is mountain biking up and down the mountain, keeping a constant speed of 10 miles per hour. Let x be the time spent mountain biking and y be the total distance biked.

J Ted bought 100 t-shirts for $5.00 each. For 20 consecutive days, he returned 5 t-shirts a day and got his money back. Let x be the number of days Ted returned t-shirts and y be the total amount spent on the t-shirts.

15. Consider this graph showing the distance run from the starting line of a race in hours.

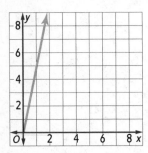

Which equation represents the distance from the starting line of someone running 1 mile per hour slower than in the graph and 7 miles from the start?

A $y = 6x + 7$

B $y = 4x + 7$

C $y = 7x + 6$

D $y = 7x + 4$

16. The temperature is 37°. It is decreasing by 1 degree every 15 minutes. Which equation models the temperature after x hours?

F $y = -x + 37$

G $y = -4x + 37$

H $y = 37x - 4$

J $y = 15x - 1$

This lesson will help you practice writing and solving a system of linear equations to find solutions to real-world problems. Use it with Core Lesson 5.4 *Solve Systems of Linear Equations* to reinforce and apply your knowledge.

Key Concept

Just like a solution of an equation is a value that makes the equation true, a solution of a system of equations is a set of values that makes all of the equations in the system true. You can solve systems of linear equations graphically by finding the point at which the graphs of the equations intersect. You can also solve systems algebraically, by using the substitution or the elimination method.

Core Skills

- Represent Real-World Problems
- Solve Pairs of Linear Equations

The Graphing Method

Solving a system of equations by graphing is a visual way to determine the solution to the problem.

Directions: Use the graphing method to answer the questions below.

1. **Consider this graph of a system of linear equations.**

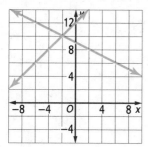

Which is the solution to the system?

A $(10, -2)$

B $(0, -2)$

C $(-2, 10)$

D $(10, 0)$

2. **Tow-A-Way charges a \$25 fee plus \$1.25 per mile to tow a car. Haul-Ur-Car charges \$1.50 per mile plus a \$15 fee to tow a car. Using the graphing method to solve, you would graph the equation for Tow-A-Way and the equation for Haul-Ur-Car, and then determine the solution from the graph. Which of these are the equations for Tow-a-Way and Haul-Ur-Car using x to represent the number of miles and y to represent the final price?**

F Tow-a-Way: $y = 25x$; Haul-Ur-Car: $y = 15x$

G Tow-a-Way: $y = 26.25x$; Haul-Ur-Car: $y = 16.50x$

H Tow-a-Way: $y = 25x + 1.25$; Haul-Ur-Car: $y = 15x + 1.5$

J Tow-a-Way: $y = 1.25x + 25$; Haul-Ur-Car: $y = 1.50x + 15$

3. Consider this system of linear equations.

$3x + 5y = 20$

$ax - 5y = 15$

Which is the value of a if the solution of the system is (5, 1)?

A -5

B -3

C 4

D 5

Directions: Use this problem to answer questions 4 and 5.

In a shopping mall, The Gummy charges \$1 per pound for gummy bears and \$1.25 for a container. The Bear charges \$2 per pound and \$0.50 for a container for gummy bears. Let x be the number of pounds and y be the total cost.

4. Which system of linear equations would be used to solve for *x* and *y*?

F The Gummy: $y = x$; The Bear: $y = 2x$

G The Gummy: $y = x + 1.25$; The Bear: $y = 2x + 0.5$

H The Gummy: $y = 0.5x + 1.25$; The Bear: $y = 2x + 1$

J The Gummy: $y = 1.25x + 1$; The Bear: $y = 0.5x + 2$

5. Which graph represents the solution to the system?

A
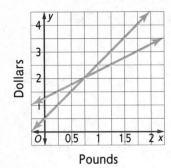

B
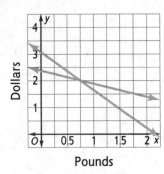

C
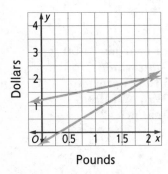

D
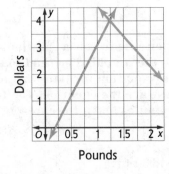

The Substitution Method

The substitution method is one algebraic way to solve a system of equations.

Directions: Use the substitution method to answer the questions below.

6. **Consider the following system of equations.**

   $4x + by = 5$

   $2x + y = 3$

   For what value of b does the system have <u>no</u> solutions?

   F   2

   G $\dfrac{5}{2}$

   H $-\dfrac{3}{5}$

   J -2

7. **Consider this system of equations.**

   $x - 4y = 1$

   $3x - y = 3$

   If the y-value of the solution is 0, what is the x-value of the solution?

   A -1

   B   0

   C $\dfrac{1}{4}$

   D   1

8. **Diana and Megan are saving money. Diana starts with \$100 and saves \$4.50 per week, while Megan starts with \$20 and saves \$12.50 per week. How much money will each of them have saved when they have saved the same amount of money after the same number of weeks? Please enter your response in the grid.**

Directions: Consider the following information to answer questions 10–12.

Water for You sells 12,500 containers of water per month. Drink Up sells 8,000 containers of water per month. After an advertising campaign, Drink Up sees an increase of 40 containers of water sales per month while Water for You has a decrease of 50 containers of water sales per month.

9. **Which is the interval in which each company sells the same number of containers?**

   A $y \leq 50$

   B $y \geq 12,500$

   C $8,000 \leq y \leq 12,500$

   D $45 \leq y \leq 50$

10. **How many months will it take for each company to sell an equal number of containers in a month? Please enter your response in the grid.**

11. **How many containers will each company sell when they are selling an equal number of containers? Please enter your response in the grid.**

12. Play World charges $25.95 for admission and $1.15 per ride. Fun Land charges $19.95 for admission and $1.25 per ride. For how many rides is the price the same, and what is that price?

F (30 rides, $60.45)

G (40 rides, $71.95)

H (50 rides, $82.45)

J (60 rides, $94.95)

 Test-Taking Tip

When trying to solve a problem that involves a system of linear equations, first determine what you are trying to solve for, and use that information to define the variables. Then, write the equations using those variables to model the data in the problem. Last, solve the system and check to make sure that the answers make sense to the problem.

The Elimination Method

The elimination method is another algebraic method used to solve a system of equations.

Directions: Use the elimination method to answer the questions below.

13. Which system of linear equations has infinite solutions?

A $4x - 4y = 12, 7x - 7y = 18$

B $4x - 4y = 12, 7x - 7y = 21$

C $4x + 4y = 10, 7x - 7y = 21$

D $4x - 4y = 12, 7x + 7y = 18$

14. Consider this system of linear equations.

$cx + 5y = -64$

$4x + 3y = -56$

What is the value of c if the solution is $(-8, -8)$?

F $\dfrac{11}{3}$

G 3

H $\dfrac{2}{3}$

J 24

15. Tickets to a school play cost $5 per student and $8 per adult. How many adult tickets were sold if 500 tickets were sold in total, and the play brought in a total of $3,700 in ticket sales? Please enter your response in the grid.

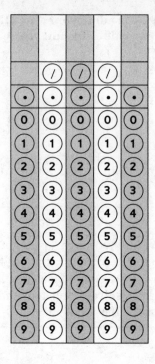

16. Robert buys 5 pairs of jeans and 9 long-sleeve t-shirts. Juan buys 2 pairs of jeans and 6 long-sleeve t-shirts. Juan spends $208, and Robert spends $376. Which system of equations can be used to find out how much each pair of jeans and each long-sleeve t-shirt cost?

   F $2x + 9y = 376, 5x + 6y = 208$

   G $5x + 2y = 208, 9x + 6y = 376$

   H $5x + 9y = 376, 2x + 6y = 208$

   J $5x + 9y = 208, 2x + 6y = 376$

17. On a 1200-mile trip, it took a plane 5 hours flying in the direction of the wind. On the return trip flying against the wind, the trip took 6 hours. How long, in hours, would the trip take flying 70 miles per hour faster in the direction of winds that are 10 miles per hour slower?

   A 3.6

   B 4

   C 4.2

   D 4.4

This lesson will help you practice recognizing functions in graphs, tables, or algebraic symbols. Use it with Core Lesson 6.1 *Identify a Function* to reinforce and apply your knowledge.

Key Concept

A function assigns exactly one output for each input. The inputs of a function are a given set, and the outputs for this function create another set. The outputs are what the function did to the set of inputs. A good way to identify a function is to use the Vertical Line Test.

Core Skills

• Use Math Tools Appropriately
• Solve Real-World Problems

Functions

Functions can represent various relationships between inputs and outputs.

Directions: Answer the questions below.

1. **Consider this graph.**

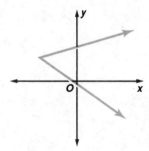

Which statement is true?

A The graph represents a function because there is more than one input for some outputs.

B The graph represents a function because there is more than one output for some inputs.

C The graph does not represent a function because there is more than one input for some outputs.

D The graph does not represent a function because there is more than one output for some inputs.

Directions: Use this information for questions 2 and 3.

The function $f(x) = 0.49x + 44.95$ represents the total cost for a company to print fliers, where x is the number of fliers printed.

2. **What is the total cost, to the nearest dollar, to print 250 fliers? Please enter your response in the grid.**

3. **Which statement is not true?**

   A The function $f(x)$ is one-to-one.

   B It costs $145.44 to print 100 fliers.

   C The output of the function $f(x)$ is the total cost.

   D The input of the function is the number of fliers printed.

Directions: Answer the questions below.

4. **Which table represents a function?**

   F

Domain	0	0	2	2
Range	3	4	5	6

   G

Domain	−1	−1	−1	−1
Range	3	4	5	6

   H

Domain	4	5	6	5
Range	3	4	5	6

   J

Domain	−3	−1	1	3
Range	3	4	5	6

5. Consider these relationships.

I. $(-2, 4), (3, 4), (6, 4)$

II.

x	4	1	0	1	4
y	2	1	0	−1	−2

III. $y = 3x - 1$

IV.

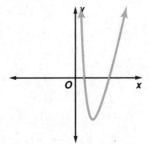

Which represent functions?

A Only II

B II and IV

C II and III

D I, III, and IV

Linear and Quadratic Functions

An example of a linear function is a set price for a number of products sold, while an example of a quadratic function is the height of an object thrown in the air.

Directions: Answer the questions below.

6. Consider these functions.

$f(x) = x^2 - 5x + 6$

$g(x) = -\frac{1}{2}x + 3$

Which statement is true?

F $f(-2) = 20; g(-2) = 4$

G $f(-2) = 12; g(-2) = 4$

H $f(-2) = 20; g(-2) = 2$

J $f(-2) = -8; g(-2) = 7$

7. If $h(-1) = 5$, which statement is true?

A The point $(1, -5)$ lies on the graph of $y = h(x)$.

B The point $(-1, 5)$ lies on the graph of $y = h^{-1}(x)$.

C The point $(5, -1)$ lies on the graph of $y = h^{-1}(x)$.

D The point $(-5, 1)$ lies on the graph of $y = h(x)$.

Test-Taking Tip

If the point (a, b) is on the graph of $f(x)$, then the point (b, a) is on the graph of the inverse function $f^{-1}(x)$.

---

8. **Consider this function.**

   $f(x) = 3x^2 - 4x + 1$

   Which statement is true?

   F $f(0) > f(1)$

   G $f(0) > f(-1)$

   H $f(1) > f(-1)$

   J $f(2) > f(-1)$

Directions: Use this information for questions 9 and 10.

The cost of buying gasoline at a particular service station is represented by the function $f(x) = 3.18x$, where x is the number of gallons of gasoline purchased.

9. **What is the cost of purchasing 5 gallons of gasoline and the cost of purchasing 12 gallons of gasoline?**

   A 5 gallons: $19.00; 12 gallons: $38.16

   B 5 gallons: $15.90; 12 gallons: $45.60

   C 5 gallons: $15.90; 12 gallons: $38.16

   D 5 gallons: $19.00; 12 gallons: $45.60

10. **Which statement describes the properties of the function?**

   F The function $f(x)$ is linear and one-to-one.

   G The function $f(x)$ is quadratic and one-to-one.

   H The function $f(x)$ is linear and not one-to-one.

   J The function $f(x)$ is quadratic and not one-to-one.

11. The height, in meters, of a ball thrown upward from the top of a building can be represented by the function $h(t) = -4.9t^2 + 19.6t + 98$ where t is the time in seconds after the ball has been thrown. What is the difference of the ball's height, in meters, at 1.5 seconds and at 2.5 seconds? Please enter your response in the grid.

Functions in the Coordinate Plane

Graphing a function is a way to visually express patterns and behaviors between inputs and outputs.

Directions: Answer the questions below.

12. **Consider this piecewise function.**

$$f(x) = \begin{cases} -5x - 3 & \text{when } x < -1 \\ 8 & \text{when } x = -1 \\ -\frac{2}{3}x + 4 & \text{when } x > -1 \end{cases}.$$

When $x = -3$, what is the value of $f(x)$? Please enter your response in the grid.

13. Consider this function.

$$f(x) = 2x^2 - 3x - 4$$

Which table represents the function?

A

x	f(x)
-2	10
0	-4
2	-2

B

x	f(x)
-2	-6
0	-4
2	-18

C

x	f(x)
-2	-2
0	-4
2	10

D

x	f(x)
-2	-2
0	-4
2	-6

14. Consider this function.

$$f(x) = 2x - 3$$

Which table represents the inverse of the function?

F

x	f⁻¹(x)
-1	-2
0	0
1	2

G

x	f⁻¹(x)
-2	-1
0	0
-1	1

H

x	f⁻¹(x)
-1	-5
0	-3
1	-1

J

x	f⁻¹(x)
-5	-1
-3	0
1	1

15. Marcus is training for a marathon. He can already run 8 miles without stopping before he starts his training. Each day he tries to increase his total mileage by 10%. Which expression represents the number of miles, *m*, that Marcus runs on day *d* of his training?

A $m = 8 + 10d$

B $m = 8 \times (1.1)^d$

C $m = 8 + 0.1d$

D $m = 8 \times 1.1 \times d$

16. Which graph is the graph of the piecewise function $h(x) \begin{cases} 4x + 5, x \leq 1 \\ -4x + 5, x > 1 \end{cases}$?

F
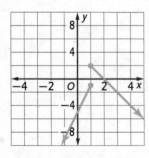

G
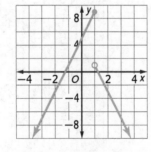

H
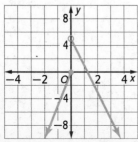

J
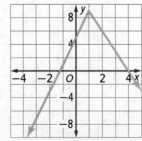

This lesson will help you practice identifying linear and quadratic functions by analyzing common differences and graphs. Use it with Core Lesson 6.2 *Identify Linear and Quadratic Functions* to reinforce and apply your knowledge.

Key Concept

Linear and quadratic functions express a relationship between two variables—one independent and the other dependent. As the independent variable changes, the dependent variable of linear functions changes at a constant rate while the dependent variable of quadratic functions does not change at a constant rate.

Core Skills

- Critique the Reasoning of Others

Evaluating Linear and Quadratic Functions

It is important to know how to evaluate linear and quadratic functions for information since they are used to model data in fields such as health, economics, and nature.

Directions: Answer the questions below.

1. **Consider this function.**

    $f(x) = 3x + 4$

    What is the common consecutive difference?

    A 1

    B 3

    C 4

    D 7

2. **Consider this function.**

    $f(x) = 2x^2 + 1$

    What is the common consecutive difference?

    F 1

    G 2

    H 4

    J 6

Directions: Use this information to answer questions 3 and 4.

John is joining a golf club that has an annual fee of $1,000 and charges $15 per round of golf.

3. **Which table represents this situation?**

A

Rounds of Golf	0	1	2	3	4	5
Total Cost	$0	$1,015	$2,030	$3,045	$4,060	$5,075

B

Rounds of Golf	0	1	2	3	4	5
Total Cost	$1,000	$985	$970	$955	$940	$925

C

Rounds of Golf	0	1	2	3	4	5
Total Cost	$0	$15	$30	$45	$60	$75

D

Rounds of Golf	0	1	2	3	4	5
Total Cost	$1,000	$1,015	$1,030	$1,045	$1,060	$1,075

4. **Which function describes the cost, C, to play r rounds of golf?**

    F $C = 1000r + 15$

    G $C = -1000r + 15$

    H $C = 15r + 1000$

    J $C = 15r - 1000$

Directions: Answer the following questions.

5. **Which graph represents the function $f(x) = x^2 + 2x - 8$?**

A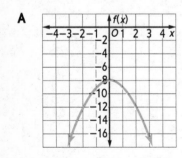

B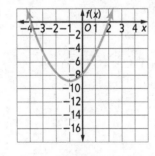

C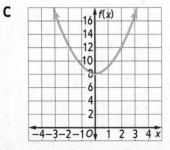

D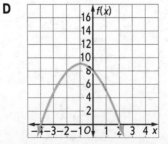

6. What is the common consecutive difference for the linear function $p(t) = 11$? Please enter your response in the grid.

7. The tables show the 2nd consecutive differences for four different functions. Which table corresponds to a function that is neither linear nor quadratic?

A

2nd Consecutive Differences	0	0	0	0	0	0

B

2nd Consecutive Differences	1	2	3	4	5	6

C

2nd Consecutive Differences	−2	−2	−2	−2	−2	−2

D

2nd Consecutive Differences	6	6	6	6	6	6

8. What is the common consecutive difference for the quadratic function $u(s) = -6s^2 + 3s + 4$?

F −3

G −12

H −18

J 3

9. For an object that has been thrown upward, the function $p(t) = -\frac{1}{2}at^2 + vt + h$ gives the object's height, in feet, t seconds after it has been thrown.

In this function

- a is the acceleration due to gravity
- v is the velocity when the object is thrown
- h is the height of the object when it is thrown

A ball is thrown into the air from a height of 32 feet with a velocity of 16 ft/sec. The acceleration due to gravity is 32 ft/sec². Which table describes the height of the ball?

A

t	0	0.5	1	1.5	2
$p(t)$	32	48	64	80	96

B

t	0	1	2	3	4
$p(t)$	32	48	64	80	96

C

t	0	0.5	1	1.5	2
$p(t)$	32	36	32	20	0

D

t	0	1	2	3	4
$p(t)$	32	64	32	16	0

10. Consider this table that gives selected values for a function $f(x)$.

x	−2	−1	0	1	2	3
$f(x)$	2	1	0	−1	−2	−3

Bobby found the first consecutive differences as shown below and concluded that the function is not linear.

x		−2	−1	0	1	2	3
$f(x)$			2	1	0	−1	−2	−3
1st Consecutive Differences			1	1	−1	−1	−1

Which of these is true?

F Bobby is correct. The function is not linear because the first consecutive differences decrease.

G Bobby is incorrect. The function is linear because the second consecutive differences are the same.

H Bobby is correct. The function is not linear because the first consecutive differences are not common.

J Bobby is incorrect. The function is linear because the first consecutive differences were calculated incorrectly and are actually common.

Recognizing Linear and Quadratic Functions

Linear and quadratic functions behave differently and learning to recognize the differences in their behavior helps you understand the information they are representing.

Directions: Use this information for questions 11 through 14.

A sports equipment company recorded data on three of their ball-launching machines. The *Pitcher* launches a baseball so users can practice hitting or catching. The *Volley* launches a tennis ball so users can practice hitting. The *Goalinator* launches soccer balls so users can practice stopping or scoring. Each machine ran for 6 minutes and the total number of balls launched was recorded each minute.

11. Consider this table that gives the data for the *Pitcher*.

Number of Minutes	0	1	2	3	4	5	6
Total Number of Balls Launched	0	4	8	12	16	20	24

Which of these is a correct description of the function that models the data?

A linear function

B quadratic function

C not a polynomial function

D polynomial function of degree 3

12. Consider this table that gives the data for the *Volley*.

Number of Minutes	0	1	2	3	4	5	6
Total Number of Balls Launched	0	1	8	27	28	36	63

Which of these is a correct description of the function that models the data?

F linear function

G quadratic function

H not a polynomial function

J polynomial function of degree 3

13. Consider this table that gives the data for the *Goalinator*.

Number of Minutes	0	1	2	3	4	5	6
Total Number of Balls Launched	0	1	4	9	16	25	36

Which of these is a correct description of the function that models the data?

A linear function

B quadratic function

C not a polynomial function

D polynomial function of degree 3

14. Which statement is false?

F The machine with data that can be modeled by a linear function dispensed the most balls after 1 minute.

G The machine for which there was no common consecutive difference dispensed the most balls after 6 minutes.

H The common consecutive difference for the *Pitcher* is equal to the common consecutive difference for the *Volley*.

J The common consecutive difference for the *Goalinator* is less than the common consecutive difference for the *Pitcher*.

 Test-Taking Tip

Use scrap paper to work problems. Tables help to organize finding consecutive differences. Also, subtracting in the same order is important; the previous y-value from the current y-value. Then, place that difference in the row that corresponds to the previous y-value.

Directions: Use this function to answer questions 15 and 16.

$$f(x) = (x^2 - 25)(x^2 - 49)$$

15. What is the common consecutive difference?
Please enter your response in the grid.

16. What type of function is $f(x)$?

F degree 3

G degree 4

H linear

J quadratic

17. What is the degree of a polynomial function that has third common consecutive differences? Please enter your response in the grid.

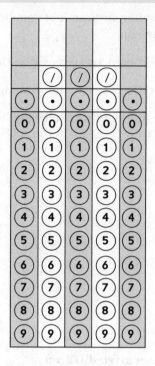

18. A question on Brenda's math test contained the graph below. Brenda was asked to determine whether the graph represents a simple interest investment or a compound interest investment.

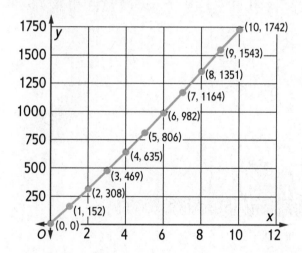

Based on the appearance of the graph, Brenda decided that the function is linear. She then concluded that because simple interest is a linear relationship, the graph must represent a simple interest investment. Which of these is true?

F Brenda's answer and her reasoning are correct.

G Brenda is incorrect. Simple interest is a linear relationship, but the function is not linear.

H Brenda is incorrect. The function is linear, but simple interest is not a linear relationship.

J Brenda's answer is correct, but her reasoning is not. The graph represents a simple interest investment, but the function is not linear.

19. For a given function, which statement is true?

A If the first consecutive differences are not common, then the second consecutive differences must be common.

B If the first consecutive differences are positive, then the function is linear.

C If the first consecutive differences are not common, then the function is quadratic.

D If the third consecutive differences are all equal to 0, then the function is quadratic or linear.

20. Consider this graph.

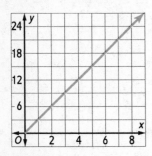

What is the common consecutive difference?

F $\frac{1}{3}$

G 1

H 2

J 3

This lesson will help you practice identifying the key features of a graph and what the features mean in a real-world situation. Use it with Core Lesson 6.3 *Identify Key Features of a Graph* to reinforce and apply your knowledge.

Key Concept	**Core Skills**
Key features that can be identified from graphs include intercepts, positive and negative intervals, increasing and decreasing intervals, relative minimums and maximums, end behavior, symmetry, and periodicity. You can sketch graphs if you know or can determine the key features to represent the visual features of the graph.	• Make Use of Structure • Gather Information

Key Features

Since graphs are used in many fields of work, it's important to know how to read and interpret their key features.

Directions: Answer the questions below.

1. **Which graph is a linear function with *x*-intercept of −4 and *y*-intercept of 5?**

A
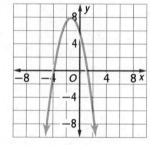

B
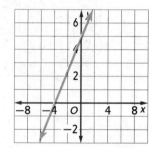

C
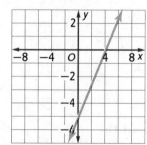

D
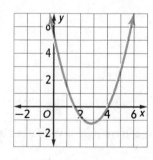

Directions: Use this graph to answer questions 2–4.

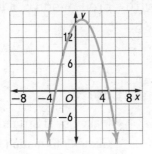

2. What value for k satisfies the equation $x = k$ for the line of symmetry in the graph? Please enter your response in the grid.

3. Which is the x-intercept(s) of the graph?

    A −3

    B −3, 5

    C 5, 15

    D 15

4. If the function given by the graph is $y = (ax + b)(cx + d)$, what is the value of the product bd?

    F −15

    G −2

    H 5

    J 15

5. Consider this graph.

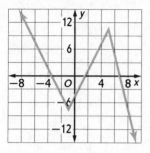

Which are the increasing and decreasing intervals for the function?

A increasing: all values for x

B increasing: $x < 5$, decreasing $x > 5$

C increasing: $-1 < x < 5$, decreasing: $x < -1$ and $x > 5$

D increasing: $x < -1$ and $x > 5$, decreasing: $-1 < x < 5$

6. Consider this factored quadratic function.

$y = (ax + b)(x - c)$

If a, b, and c are all positive, what can you say about the end behavior of the graph of the function?

F The left end is increasing indefinitely, and the right end is decreasing indefinitely.

G The left end is increasing indefinitely, and the right end is increasing indefinitely.

H The left end is decreasing indefinitely, and the right end is decreasing indefinitely.

J The left end is decreasing indefinitely, and the right end is increasing indefinitely.

Directions: Consider this graph to answer questions 7 and 8.

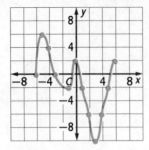

7. What is the sum of the relative maxima in the
    graph? Please enter your response in the grid.

8. What is the difference between the largest
    relative maximum and the smallest relative
    minimum in the graph? Please enter your
    response in the grid.

9. **Consider this graph.**

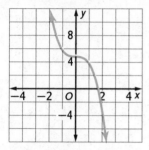

Which type of symmetry does the graph have?

A origin

B rotational

C x-axis

D y-axis

10. **Which is the equation for a parabola with a vertex at $(2, -4)$? The vertex form of a quadratic equation is $y = a(x - h)^2 + k$, where (h, k) is the vertex of the graph.**

F $y = 2x^2 - 12x + 22$

G $y = -4x^2 - 16x - 13$

H $y = 3x^2 - 12x + 8$

J $y = 3x^2 + 12x + 16$

11. **The path of a football thrown in the air drawn on a graph has y-axis symmetry across the line $x = 3$. Which could be the equation that describes the path of the football?**

A $y = -2x^2 + 12x - 10$

B $y = -2x^2 + 16x - 32$

C $y = 2x^2 + 12x + 10$

D $y = 2x^2 + 12x + 18$

Use Key Features to Draw a Graph

Being able to create graphs when given specific features can help you visually communicate data and information.

Directions: Answer the questions below.

12. Which quadratic graph has the key features of x-intercepts of -4 and 4, y-intercept of -8, symmetrical about the y-axis, and extends up indefinitely at both ends?

F
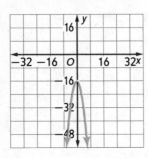

G
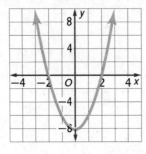

H
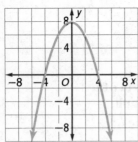

J
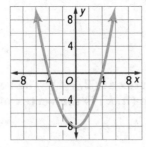

13. Which linear graph has the key features of x-intercept of 3, y-intercept of 2, and extends down indefinitely?

A
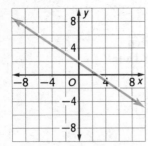

B
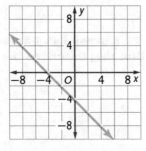

C
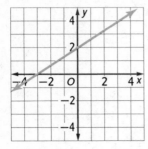

D
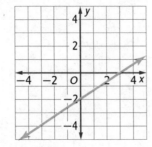

14. Which graph of a function has relative maximums at y-values 0 and -1, a relative minimum at y-value -3, an x-intercept of 2, and extends down indefinitely in both directions?

F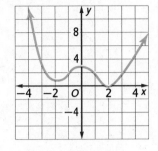

G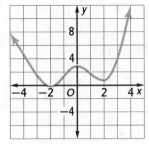

H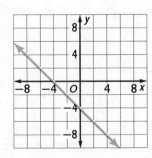

J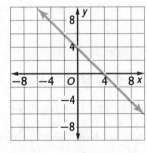

✓ Test-Taking Tip

When sketching a graph with specific features, it helps to plot points for all intercepts, draw arrows for end behavior, and then connect the points and arrowheads, paying attention to any maximums and minimums.

---

15. Which graph has an x-intercept that is the opposite of the y-intercept, and extends upward indefinitely?

A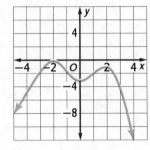

B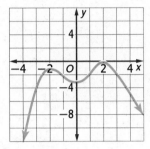

C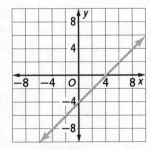

D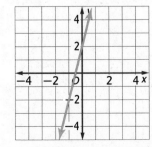

16. Which graph of a function has relative maximum at *y*-value 7, a *y*-intercept of 5, increases for *x* < 1 and decreases for *x* > 1, and extends down indefinitely in both directions?

F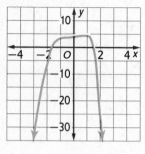

G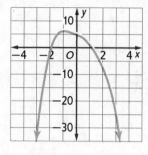

H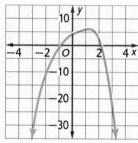

J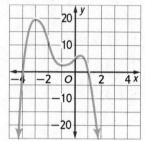

17. Given the function $y = mx + b$ for a line, which of the following must be true of *m* and *b* if the function has a positive *x*-intercept and a negative *y*-intercept?

A $m > 0; b > 0$

B $m > 0; b < 0$

C $m < 0; b > 0$

D $m < 0; b < 0$

18. The function $y = x^2 + 5x - 12$ is plotted on a graph. What must be true of its end behavior?

F The graph will extend up to the left and up to the right indefinitely.

G The graph will extend up to the left and down to the right indefinitely.

H The graph will extend down to the left and up to the right indefinitely.

J The graph will extend down to the left and down to the right indefinitely.

This lesson will help you practice comparing properties of two functions when they are each represented in a different way such as algebraically, graphically, numerically in tables, or by verbal description. Use it with Core Lesson 6.4 *Compare Functions* to reinforce and apply your knowledge.

Key Concept

Functions can be represented in many ways—graphs, tables, equations, verbal descriptions, and so on. To compare two or more functions represented in different ways, you will have to use the information given in each representation to determine key features that can be compared.

Core Skills

- Use Ratio and Rate Reasoning
- Make sense of Problems

Compare Proportional Relationships

This section will help you practice comparing key features of two proportions represented in different ways such as graphs, tables, equations, and verbal descriptions.

Directions: Answer the question below.

1. **The average calories burned in 30 minutes of jogging for a woman is 210. Consider this table that shows the average calories burned per minute of biking for a woman:**

Minutes Biking	Calories Used
1	8
2	16
3	24

Which of these statements is false?

A Women use 420 calories jogging for an hour.

B Women use 30 calories for every 4 minutes of biking.

C Women burn more calories biking for 30 minutes than jogging for 30 minutes.

D Women burn the same number of calories by biking for 70 minutes or jogging for 80 minutes.

Directions: Use this information to answer questions 2 and 3.

Two publishing companies are interested in publishing Kimberly's book. Sell Your Book Company will pay Kimberly 20 cents for every book sold. The E-Your Book Company will pay Kimberly according to the function represented by the graph.

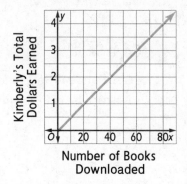

2. **How many books must Kimberly sell through E-Your Book Company to earn $20? Please enter your response in the grid.**

3. **Which statement has incorrect information?**

    A Kimberly will earn $12 from Sell Your Book if 60 books are sold.

    B Kimberly will earn $3 from E-Your Book if 60 books are downloaded.

    C Sell Your Book will pay Kimberly more per book sold than E-Your Book will pay per book downloaded.

    D Kimberly will earn the same amount from both companies when 100 books are sold or downloaded.

4. **Consider this information that Brendan and Ann were given in class:**

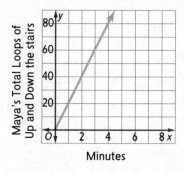

Minutes	Dana's Total Loops
1	10
2	20
3	30
4	40

The graph and table show how many loops of up and down the stairs Dana and Maya can run in a certain amount of time. Brendan and Ann are to find which one of the girls is faster.

Minutes	Dana's Total Loops	1st Common Difference
1	10	
2	20	10
3	30	10
4	40	10

This is Brendan's solution:

Using the table, Dana runs 10 loops per minute.

Using the graph, $\frac{40-20}{2-1} = 20$, which is the slope. Therefore, Maya runs 20 loops per minute.

Maya runs more loops so Maya is faster.

This is Ann's solution:

Maya runs $\frac{1}{20}$ of a loop in a minute.

Dana runs $\frac{1}{10}$ of a loop in a minute.

Dana runs more of a loop in a minute so Dana is faster.

Which is an <u>incorrect</u> statement?

F Ann should not have used a ratio to determine who was faster.

G Ann did not find the faster runner because she inverted the ratio.

H Brendan correctly found the common difference and slope. His conclusion is correct.

J Ann is correct in her statement that $\frac{1}{10}$ of a loop in a minute is faster than $\frac{1}{20}$ of a loop in a minute.

✓ Test-Taking Tip

To find the inverse of a function, use the order of operations to solve for the other variable.

Compare Linear Functions

This section will help you practice comparing linear functions represented in different ways such as graphs, tables, equations, and verbal descriptions.

Directions: Use this information to answer questions 5–7.

Two grocery stores sell almonds by the pound. Fresh Day grocery store sells almonds for $3 a pound plus a container fee of $2. Friendly Earth grocery store sells almonds according to the prices in the table.

Pounds of Almonds	1	2	3	4
Total Cost at Friendly Earth	$5	$7	$9	$11

5. **Buddy's Market wants to set their price for almonds so that the cost for 10 pounds is the average of Fresh Day and Friendly Earth groceries. Buddy's Market will have no container fee. What should be Buddy Market's set price per pound?**

   A $2.30

   B $2.50

   C $2.75

   D $3

6. **Which of the following could be used to find the number of pounds of almonds bought, p, from Fresh Day grocery given the amount spent, s?**

   F $p = \dfrac{s-3}{2}$

   G $p = \dfrac{s-2}{3}$

   H $p = \dfrac{s}{2} - 3$

   J $p = \dfrac{s}{3} - 2$

7. **How many dollars do almonds cost per pound at Friendly Earth? Please enter your response in the grid.**

Directions: Use this information to answer questions 8 and 9.

Lisa and George are driving to the other side of their state. They both enter the highway at different mile markers but are driving at a constant speed in the same direction. They will both cross the state line after mile marker 0. Lisa's trip is represented by the graph. George's trip is represented by the table of values.

Lisa's Trip

Mile Marker on Highway
400
300 (0, 300)
(1, 230)
200 (2, 160)
100

O 2 4 6 8

Hours Driving

George's Trip

Hours Driving	Mile Marker on Highway
1	190
2	130
3	70
4	10

8. **At what mile marker on the highway did George start his trip? Please enter your response in the grid.**

9. **Which statement is false?**

A It took Lisa 4 hours to cross the state line.

B Lisa is driving 10 miles per hour faster than George.

C After 4 hours of driving, George is at mile marker 10.

D Both slopes are negative because distance is decreasing as they approach mile marker 0.

Directions: Answer the questions below.

10. Barbara and Susan are evaluating job proposals in their field. They each compare one of their proposals. Barbara's was given to her in the form of a graph. Susan's was given to her in the form of a table of values. They are both full-time jobs so an hourly paid job is 40 hours a week. Consider the graph, table, and conclusions:

Barbara's Job Proposal

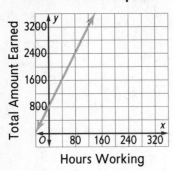

Hours Working

Susan's Job Proposal

Weeks Working	Total Amount Earned
1	2,000
2	3,000
3	4,000
4	5,000
5	6,000
6	7,000

Barbara claims that she will get paid $1,600 a week.

Susan claims that she will get a weekly salary of $1,000 and she gets an annual bonus of $1,000.

Which is an incorrect critique of their job proposal interpretations?

F Susan is correct. She will get paid a weekly salary of $1,000.

G Barbara also gets paid an initial amount. This amount equals $800.

H Based on a 40 hour work week, Barbara is correct that she will get paid $1,600 a week.

J Susan does get paid an initial amount of $1,000 so it could be an annual bonus or it might be a signing bonus. If she has not already, she needs to ask what this $1,000 is.

11. A company wants to compare the cost of manufacturing two of their new items. Item One costs $2,300 to get the plant ready for its production and costs $12 an item to manufacture. Item Two's total cost is represented by the equation $C(x) = 25x + 1,100$ where x is the number of items manufactured. Which statement is incorrect with respect to the cost of these two items?

A Item One's initial set up fee cost more than Item Two's.

B Item Two costs more per item to manufacture than Item One.

C Item Two costs less than Item One when 50 items are manufactured.

D Item One costs more than Item Two when 100 items are manufactured.

Compare Quadratic Functions

This section will help you practice comparing quadratic functions represented in different ways such as graphs, tables, equations, and verbal descriptions.

Directions: Use this information to answer questions 12–14.

Mr. Bott hits his golf ball off an elevated tee 64 feet from the ground. The height of his golf ball after t seconds is $H(t) = -16t^2 + 120t + 64$. Mrs. Bott hits her golf ball off an elevated tee, and the height of her golf ball after t seconds is represented by the graph.

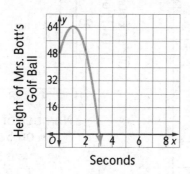

12. What maximum height will Mrs. Bott's golf ball reach?

F 1 foot

G 16 feet

H 48 feet

J 64 feet

13. Which statement incorrectly describes the flight of Mr. Bott's golf ball compared to Mrs. Bott's?

A Mrs. Bott's golf ball stayed in the air longer.

B Mr. Bott's golf ball travels higher than Mrs. Bott's golf ball.

C Mrs. Bott's golf ball hits the ground before Mr. Bott's golf ball.

D Mr. Bott's golf ball reaches a greater maximum height than Mrs. Bott's golf ball.

14. After how many seconds will Mr. Bott's golf ball hit the ground?

F −0.5 seconds

G 3 seconds

H 8 seconds

J 64 seconds

Directions: Use this information to answer questions 15 and 16.

Consider the potential weekly profits of an older book and a newer book in the graph and table where x is the number of weeks the book is on sale and y is the total profit for the week, in thousands of dollars.

Number of Weeks on Sale (x)	Newer Book's Weekly Total Profit (y)
9	0
11	18
13	28
14	30
14.5	30.25
15	30
16	28
18	18
20	0

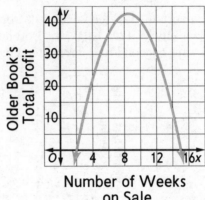

15. **How much potential weekly profit does the newer book make after being on sale for 16 weeks?**

    A 0

    B $5,000

    C $28,000

    D $30,250

16. **Which statement makes a false comparison between the old and new book's potential weekly profits?**

    F The older book will make a profit longer than the newer book.

    G The older book will start making a profit after the newer book.

    H The older book will be making more of a profit during week 11 than the newer book.

    J It will take the newer book longer to reach its maximum potential weekly profit than the older book.

This lesson will help you practice calculating perimeter and area of 2-dimensional shapes. Use it with Core Lesson 7.1 *Compute Perimeter and Area of Polygons* to reinforce and apply your knowledge.

Key Concept	Core Skills
Formulas can be used to find the perimeter and area of polygons.	• Calculate Area • Perform Operations

Rectangles

Rectangles are a type of polygon with four right angles.

Directions: Answer the questions below.

1. **Your driveway is 35 feet long and 24 feet wide. Blacktop sealer costs $18.50 per tub, and it covers 420 square feet. Which of these will be the cost to seal your driveway with two coats of sealer?**

   A $18.50

   B $37.00

   C $55.50

   D $74.00

2. **Consider this rectangle.**

   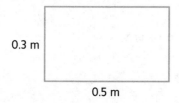

   0.3 m

   0.5 m

   What is the area, in square meters, of the rectangle? Please enter your response in the grid.

3. Which would be the most appropriate unit of measurement for a painter estimating the surface area of a wall?

   A cubic feet

   B square feet

   C cubic inches

   D square inches

4. Eastbridge High School is 80 feet long and 52 feet wide. How many times must a student run around the school in order to have run a mile? (1 mile = 5,280 ft.)

   F 10

   G 20

   H 25

   J 40

5. A box measures 10 inches in height, 18 inches across the front, and 12 inches front to back. Ribbon is being wrapped up the front face, across the top, down the back face, and under the bottom. How much ribbon, in inches, is needed to complete one time around the box?

   A 32

   B 38

   C 40

   D 44

6. A cutting board is 30 centimeters wide. How long, in centimeters, must it be to have an area of 1,140 square centimeters?

   F 28

   G 38

   H 42

   J 540

7. A rectangle has as many square inches of area as it has inches of perimeter. The rectangle is 6 inches long. How wide, in inches, is the rectangle?

   A 2

   B 3

   C 4

   D 8

8. A rectangle has an area of 24 square centimeters. Each side length is a whole number of centimeters. What is the greatest perimeter the rectangle can have, in centimeters? Please enter your response in the grid.

9. Pleasantville is 17 miles due north of Oakton, Starburg is 23 miles due east of Pleasantville, and Buckbridge is 17 miles due south of Starburg. How far, in miles, do you travel going from Oakton to Pleasantville to Starburg to Buckbridge and back to Oakton?

A   40

B   57

C   80

D   97

Triangles

Triangles are the building blocks of many weight-bearing structures because they are inherently strong and rigid.

Directions: Answer the questions below.

10. The base of a triangular sail will be 3 meters wide. How tall, in meters, must the sail be to have an area of 7.5 square meters?

F   3

G   4.5

H   5

J   10.5

11. Consider this triangle.

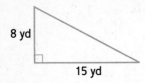

8 yd

15 yd

What is the perimeter, in yards, of the triangle?

A 23

B 38

C 40

D 60

 Test-Taking Tip

If you are asked to find a missing side length of a polygon based on its area or perimeter, first write out the formula for the area or perimeter of that polygon. Then, substitute the information you have and solve for the missing side length.

---

12. Consider this triangle.

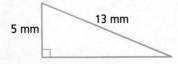

13 mm

5 mm

What is the area, in square millimeters, of the triangle? Please enter your response in the grid.

13. An isosceles triangle has one side 8 inches long and another side 3 inches long. What is the shortest possible perimeter, in inches? Hint: Try to draw all possible solutions.

A 11

B 15

C 19

D 24

14. Consider this triangle.

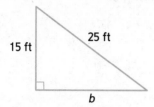

15 ft

25 ft

b

What is the length, in feet, of side *b*?

F 20

G 40

H 60

J 400

15. Consider this triangle.

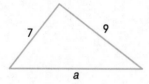

7

9

a

The perimeter of the triangle is 27 units. What is the length, in units, of *a*? Please enter your response in the grid.

16. A helicopter flying at 120 mph takes off at noon and flies south for 180 miles and then west 240 miles before returning to its original position. At what time will it return to its original position?

F 3:30 p.m.

G 4:30 p.m.

H 5:30 p.m.

J 6:00 p.m.

17. A right triangle has one leg that measures 8 inches and an area of 24 square inches. All the sides have whole number lengths. What is the length, in inches, of the longest side?

A 8

B 10

C 12

D 16

Parallelograms and Trapezoids

A parallelogram has two sets of opposite parallel sides while a trapezoid has one set of opposite parallel sides.

Directions: Answer the questions below.

18. Consider this parallelogram crosswalk.

25 ft

7 ft

What is the area, in square feet, of the crosswalk?

F 84

G 168

H 175

J 300

19. A flowerbed is to be laid out in the shape of a trapezoid. One base will be 3 meters and the height will be 5 meters. What will be the length, in meters, of the other base so that the flowerbed will have an area of 35 square meters?

A 4

B 7

C 9

D 11

20. Consider this parallelogram.

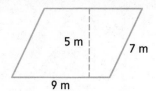

What is the perimeter, in meters, of the parallelogram?

F 16

G 28

H 32

J 45

21. Two 9-inch poles and two 15-inch poles are attached with flexible joints to make a rectangular frame. How much more area, in square inches, does the frame contain when it is in Position A than in Position B?

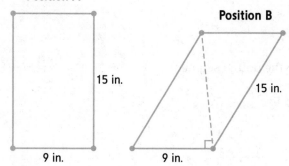

A 13.5

B 27

C 108

D 135

22. Consider this parallelogram.

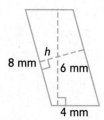

What is the length, in millimeters, of the line segment labeled *h*?

F 3

G 5.67

H 6

J 12

23. Consider this trapezoid.

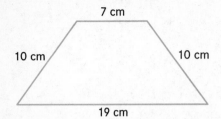

If the area of the trapezoid is 104 square centimeters, what is the height, in centimeters, of the trapezoid? Please enter your response in the grid.

Directions: Questions 24 and 25 are based on the information below.

Consider the trapezoid below. The segment of length x is parallel to the dotted segment.

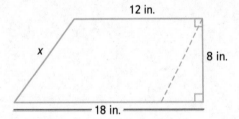

24. What is the length, in inches, of side x?

F 8

G 9

H 10

J 12

25. What is the area, in square inches, of the polygon?

A 96

B 120

C 144

D 180

This lesson will help you practice using formulas for the circumference and area of a circle. Use it with Core Lesson 7.2 *Compute Circumference and Area of Circles* to reinforce and apply your knowledge.

Key Concept	Core Skills
You can use formulas to find the circumference and area of circles.	• Perform Operations • Calculate Area

Circumference

The circumference of a circle is the distance around the edge of the circle, similar to the perimeter of a polygon.

Directions: Answer the questions below.

1. A circular racetrack is 600 feet in diameter. To the nearest foot, what is the circumference of the racetrack? Use 3.14 as an approximation for π.

   A 942

   B 1,884

   C 2,826

   D 3,768

2. Consider this circular park below.

   Entrance

   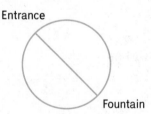

   Fountain

   One path leads around the border of the park, and another path leads straight through the center. The path through the center from the entrance to the fountain is 800 meters long. How much longer, to the nearest meter, is the path from the entrance to the fountain by going around the border of the park? Use 3.14 as an approximation for π.

   F 228

   G 456

   H 1,256

   J 2,512

3. A bicycle wheel makes 475 revolutions to travel 1 kilometer. To the tenth of a meter, what is the diameter of the wheel? (1 km = 1000 m) Use 3.14 as an approximation for π.

A 0.3

B 0.7

C 1.05

D 1.4

4. Consider this diagram that shows a large gear and a small gear.

In the time that it takes the large gear to turn 15 times, how many times does the small gear turn? Use 3.14 as an approximation for π. Please enter your response in the grid.

5. A stone is dropped into a pool. The water ripples outward at a rate of 2 ft/sec. What is the circumference of the ripple, to the nearest foot, after 15 seconds? Use 3.14 as an approximation for π.

A 47

B 94

C 141

D 188

Area

The area of a circle is the two-dimensional space inside its circumference.

Directions: Answer the questions below.

6. **What is the area, in square inches, of a circle whose diameter is 22 inches?**

    F 11π

    G 121π

    H 363π

    J 484π

 Test-Taking Tip

It is easy to confuse the radius and the diameter of a circle when making calculations, since both are used to solve problems. The diameter or the radius can be used to find the circumference. The radius is needed to find the area. Note whether you are given the radius or the diameter and, if necessary, convert from one to the other by multiplying or dividing by 2 before making further calculations.

7. **A chef has been preparing sushi on a circular table with a diameter of 15 inches. She decides she needs a table with at least twice the area of her current table. What is the minimum diameter, to the nearest tenth of an inch, of her new table? Use 3.14 as an approximation for π. Please enter your response in the grid.**

8. Gregor is covering the top of a circular box with glitter as a stage prop for a play. The box has a radius of 10 inches. Each packet of glitter covers an area of 12 square inches. What is the minimum number of glitter packets Gregor will need for this task? Use 3.14 as an approximation for π. Please enter your response in the grid.

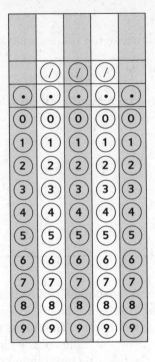

9. Consider this diagram.

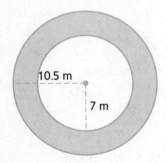

10.5 m

7 m

What is the area, to the nearest square meter, of the unshaded part of the diagram? Use 3.14 as an approximation for π.

A 154

B 192

C 297

D 346

10. What is the area, in square centimeters, of a circle that has a circumference of 18π centimeters?

F 36π

G 64π

H 81π

J 96π

11. Stefan made a pizza with a diameter of 10 inches. He calculated the area of the pizza to be 100π square inches. Which of these describes why Stefan's answer is incorrect?

   A He forgot to square the radius.

   B He did not use an approximation for π.

   C He did not use half the diameter to find the radius.

   D He confused the formulas for circumference and area.

Find Radius or Diameter

The formulas for circumference and area can also be used to find a radius or a diameter.

Directions: Answer the questions below.

12. A Ferris wheel has a circumference of 126 feet and the lowest seat is 10 feet off the ground. To the nearest foot, how high are you off the ground when the seat is halfway through a revolution? Use 3.14 as an approximation for π.

   F 20

   G 30

   H 50

   J 80

13. After running 4 laps around her high school's circular track, Sonya had completed a mile. To the nearest foot, what is the radius of the track? (1 mi = 5,280 ft) Use 3.14 as an approximation for π.

   A 210

   B 220

   C 420

   D 840

14. Each pound of grass seed covers 400 square feet. What is the radius, to the nearest foot, of the largest circular lawn that can be planted with 2 pounds of grass seed? Use 3.14 as an approximation for π.

   F 11

   G 14

   H 16

   J 20

15. Janna used 2 cups of flour to make the dough for a pizza with an 8-inch diameter. What is the diameter, in inches, of the largest pizza she can form using the dough made from 4.5 cups of flour?

A 10.5

B 12

C 12.5

D 18

16. Consider this heart-shaped figure.

The area of the figure is 28.6 square centimeters. What is the side length, to the nearest centimeter, of the square? Use 3.14 as an approximation for π.

F 3

G 4

H 5

J 6

This lesson will help you practice calculating surface area and volume of three-dimensional objects. Use it with Core Lesson 7.3 *Compute Surface Area and Volume* to reinforce and apply your knowledge.

Key Concept	Core Skills
The volume of a three-dimensional object is the number of cubic units it takes to fill the object. The surface area of a three-dimensional object is the number of square units it takes to cover all sides of the object.	• Calculate Volume • Calculate Surface Area

Rectangular Prisms

Many boxes are shaped like rectangular prisms, so it's useful to know how to find surface area and volume for them.

Directions: Answer the question below.

1. The volume of a rectangular prism is given by the expression $x^3 + 6x^2 + 9x$. If the height is x and the length of each base can be represented by a binomial, what is the surface area of the prism?

   A $2x^2 + 4(x + 3)^2$

   B $4x(x + 3) + 2(x + 3)^2$

   C $x^2(x + 3)^2 + (x + 3)^4$

   D $x^4 + x^2(x + 3)^2$

2. A container shaped like a rectangular prism can hold 864 cubic millimeters. The length of the container is 3 times the width, and the sum of the length and width is 16 mm. What is the height of the container? Please enter your response in the grid.

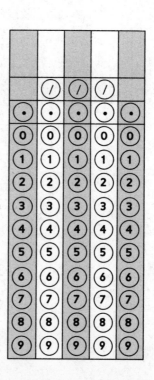

3. A cement patio, in the form of a rectangular prism, is being poured with dimensions 50 feet by 16 feet by 18 inches. An 80-pound bag of cement mix makes 0.6 cubic feet of cement. How many pounds of cement mix is necessary to fill the patio?

    A 1,120,000

    B 160,000

    C 64,000

    D 9,600

Directions: Use this information to answer questions 4 and 5.

A box shaped like a rectangular prism has a width of 8.5 inches, a length of 9.5 inches, and a height of 14 inches.

4. What is the volume, in cubic inches, of the box?

    F 252

    G 565.25

    H 1,130.5

    J 2,261

5. What is the surface area, in square inches, of the box? Please enter your response in the grid.

Cylinders and Prisms

Prisms and cylinders both have heights, but the base of a prism is a polygon while the base of a cylinder is a circle.

Directions: Use this information to answer questions 6 and 7. Round each answer to the nearest tenth. Use 3.14 as an approximation for π.

A can of food in the shape of a cylinder has a diameter of 8 centimeters and a height of 20 centimeters.

6. **Which expression shows the approximate number of cubic centimeters that the can is able to hold?**

    F $(3.14)(8)^2(20)$

    G $(3.14)(4)^2(20)$

    H $(3.14)(8)(20)$

    J $(3.14)(4)(20)$

7. **Approximately how many square centimeters of labeling are needed to cover the can excluding the two bases? Please enter your response in the grid.**

Directions: Use this information to answer questions 8 and 9.

The right triangle base of a triangular prism has side lengths of 8 inches, 15 inches, and 17 inches. The prism has a height of 20 inches.

8. **Which expression represents the volume of the prism in cubic inches?**

   F $\frac{1}{2}(8)(15)(17)$

   G $\frac{1}{2}(8)(17)(20)$

   H $\frac{1}{2}(15)(17)(20)$

   J $\frac{1}{2}(8)(15)(20)$

9. **A second triangular prism has a volume of 14,400 cubic inches, is 3 times the height of the first triangular prism, and the side lengths of the base are b times the side lengths of the first triangle described above. What is the value of b?**

   A 2

   B 4

   C 6

   D 12

Directions: Use this information to answer questions 10 and 11.

A tent is shaped like a triangular prism with a length of 4 feet. The front and rear tent flaps are shaped like triangles, each with a base of 3 feet, a height of 2 feet, and two side lengths of 2.5 feet as shown in the diagram.

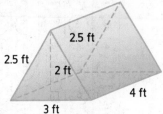

10. **What is the volume of the tent in cubic feet?**

   F 3

   G 6

   H 12

   J 18

11. **How much material, in square feet, was necessary to construct the tent?**

   A 18

   B 38

   C 42

   D 54

Pyramids, Cones, and Spheres

Pyramids and cones are both solids with a height and a vertex, but the base of a pyramid is a polygon and the base of a cone is a circle.

Directions: Use this information to answer questions 12 and 13. Use 3.14 as an approximation for π.

A square pyramid has a base with side lengths of 12 centimeters and a height of 8 centimeters.

12. What is the volume of the pyramid in cubic centimeters?

   F 96

   G 144

   H 288

   J 384

13. What is the surface area of the pyramid in square centimeters?

   A 264

   B 384

   C 528

   D 624

Directions: Use this information to answer questions 14 and 15. Use 3.14 as an approximation for π. Round your answers to the nearest tenth, when applicable.

An inflatable ice cream cone has a diameter of 10 inches and a height of 12 inches.

14. Approximately how much gas, in cubic inches, is needed to inflate the cone?

   F 314

   G 942

   H 1,256

   J 1,884

15. What is the approximate surface area of the cone in square inches?

   A 219.8

   B 266.9

   C 282.6

   D 690.8

Directions: Answer the question below.

16. **Approximately how many pounds of water are needed to inflate a spherical water balloon to a diameter of 10 inches? Round the answer to the nearest hundredth. Use 3.14 as an approximation for π and 0.58 ounces per square inch as an approximation of the density of water.**

   F 60.70

   G 30.35

   H 18.97

   J 3.77

 Test-Taking Tip

A cross-section is the intersection of a 3D object and a 2D plane. The most familiar cross-sections of an object are its faces, but a plane can intersect the object at different places. To visualize the shape of the cross-section, think of what that portion of the object would look like as a slice that is cut out.

Directions: Consider this figure to answer questions 17 and 18.

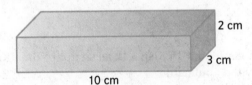

17. **What would be the shape of the cross section that is made by cutting off one of the corners of the prism?**

   A triangle

   B square

   C rectangle

   D hexagon

18. **What is the area, in square centimeters of a cross-section of the prism that is parallel to the base?**

   F 6

   G 26

   H 30

   J 60

This lesson will help you practice analyzing dimensions of composite figures by breaking them into their component shapes. Use it with Core Lesson 7.4 *Compute Perimeter, Area, Surface Area, and Volume of Composite Figures* to reinforce and apply your knowledge.

Key Concept

To find the area of a composite figure, add the area of each figure in the composite. To find the perimeter, add pieces of the perimeter of each figure. Similarly, to find the volume of a composite solid, add the volume of each solid. To find the surface area, add parts of each solid's surface area.

Core Skills

- Calculate Area
- Make Sense of Problems

2-Dimensional Figures

In the real world, you may need to find the area and perimeter of two-dimensional composite shapes, such as the floor plan of an apartment or an odd-shaped backyard.

Directions: Consider this diagram to answer questions 1 and 2.

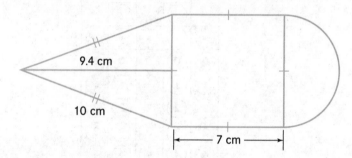

1. **What is the approximate perimeter of the figure in centimeters? Use 3.14 as an approximation for π.**

   A 44.99

   B 55.98

   C 69.98

   D 77.96

2. **What is the approximate area of the figure in square centimeters? Use 3.14 as an approximation for π. Round to the nearest hundredth.**

   F 101.13

   G 115.23

   H 120.37

   J 158.83

Directions: Consider this diagram to answer questions 3 and 4.

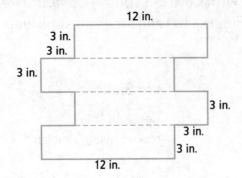

3. **What is the perimeter, in inches, of the figure?**

   A 45

   B 48

   C 54

   D 66

4. **What is the area, in square inches, of the figure? Please enter your response in the grid.**

Directions: Consider this diagram of the shape of a garden. Use the diagram to answer questions 5 and 6. Using 3.14 as an approximation for π.

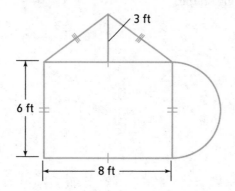

5. **Plastic lining costs $6 per foot. How much will it cost to place plastic lining around the garden to the nearest dollar? Please enter your response in the grid.**

6. **A landscaping service charges $10 per square foot to cover ground with soil and mulch. Approximately how much will it cost to cover the entire garden with soil and mulch?**

   F $334.20

   G $709.90

   H $741.30

   J $1,002.60

Volume of 3-Dimensional Solids

Knowing how to calculate the volume of a composite figure is useful whenever you need to find the capacity of something made up of more than one shape.

Directions: Answer the questions below.

7. **Consider this figure.**

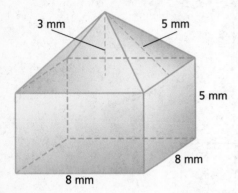

3 mm   5 mm

5 mm

8 mm

8 mm

What is the volume of the figure to the nearest mm³?

A 324

B 341

C 384

D 405

8. A square pyramid with a height of 8 centimeters is stacked on a cube. The side of the cube is $2\frac{1}{2}$ times greater than the height of the pyramid. What is the volume of the composite figure to the nearest cubic centimeter?

F 8,067

G 9,067

H 11,200

J 16,000

9. A vitamin capsule has the shape of a cylinder with a hemisphere on each end. The radius of each hemisphere is 2 mm. The height of the cylinder part of the capsule is 10 mm. What is the approximate volume of the capsule? Round to the nearest cubic millimeter. Use 3.14 as an approximation for π.

A 92

B 109

C 142

D 159

10. A farmer has a silo that is shaped like a cylinder with a hemisphere on top. The cylinder part of the silo is 45 feet tall and the height of the hemisphere is $\frac{1}{3}$ the height of the silo. Approximately how many cubic feet of grain can the farmer store in the silo? Use 3.14 as an approximation for π and round to the nearest whole number. Please enter your response in the grid.

11. A perfume bottle is packaged in a box shaped like a cone sitting on top of a cylinder with a radius of 5 cm. The height of the cylinder is 24 cm and the height of the cone is $\frac{1}{2}$ the height of the cylinder. What is the approximate volume of the box to the nearest cubic centimeter? Use 3.14 as an approximation for π.

A   439

B   753

C   2,198

D   3,770

12. If the radius of a cylinder is tripled, what happens to the volume of the cylinder?

F   The volume is tripled.

G   The volume is 9 times the original volume.

H   The volume is 27 times the original volume.

J   The volume is increased by 3 cubic units.

Surface Area of 3-Dimensional Solids

You may need to calculate surface area when you do real-world tasks such as painting a house or wrapping a gift.

Directions: Answer the questions below.

13. What is the approximate surface area of the figure below, in square millimeters?

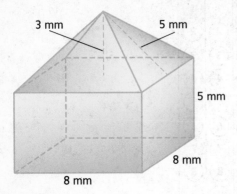

3 mm   5 mm

5 mm

8 mm

8 mm

A 240

B 272

C 304

D 444

14. A farmer owns a silo that is shaped like a cylinder with a hemisphere on top. The cylinder part of the silo is 45 feet tall and the height of the hemisphere is $\frac{1}{3}$ the height of the silo. The farmer wants to paint the exterior of the silo excluding the base of the cylinder. If one gallon of paint covers 400 square feet, how many gallons of paint does the farmer need for one coat? Use 3.14 as an approximation for π.

F 11

G 14

H 15

J 18

15. A vitamin capsule has the shape of a cylinder with a hemisphere on each end. The radius of each hemisphere is 2 mm. The height of the cylinder part of the capsule is 10 mm. The vitamin manufacturer puts a coating around each capsule to make it easier to swallow. Approximately how many square millimeters of coating are necessary? Round to the nearest whole number and use 3.14 as an approximation for π.

A 126

B 151

C 176

D 201

16. A department store is wrapping perfume to sell for the holidays. A perfume bottle is packaged in a box shaped like a cone sitting on top of a cylinder with a radius of 5 cm. The height of the cylinder is 24 cm and the height of the cone is the $\frac{1}{2}$ height of the cylinder. How many rolls of wrapping paper would be needed to wrap 100 bottles if each roll has 4 square meters of paper? Use 3.14 as an approximation for π.

F 1

G 2

H 3

J 4

 Test-Taking Tip

Many solids can be built by taking a 2-dimensional shape and rotating it about an axis. For example, the triangle shown rotated 360° about its long leg produces the cone.

---

17. The rectangle is rotated 360° about the dotted line. What is the volume of the solid, in cubic inches, that is produced by the rotation?

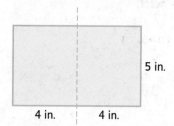

A 20π

B 26π

C 40π

D 80π

18. Which rotation of a 2-dimensional object about the given line produces a sphere?

F   rotated by 360°

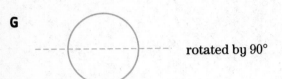

G   rotated by 90°

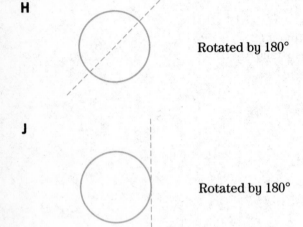

H   Rotated by 180°

J   Rotated by 180°

19. A Rubik's® Cube is a toy originally designed for children that has gained popularity among people of all ages. The toy is a cube that is made from smaller pieces with 9 smaller square faces on each different colored side. Each smaller face is approximately $\frac{3}{4}$ inch in length. What is the total surface area of the entire cube, in square inches?

A $5\frac{1}{16}$

B $13\frac{1}{2}$

C $30\frac{3}{8}$

D $45\frac{9}{16}$

This lesson will help you practice describing and summarizing sets of numbers, and determining common measures of tendency, including mean, median, mode, and range. Use it with Core Lesson 8.1 *Calculate Measures of Central Tendency* to reinforce and apply your knowledge.

Key Concept

A measure of central tendency is a number that can be used to summarize a group of numbers. Mean, median, and mode are measures of central tendency calculated in different ways.

Core Skills

* Interpret Data Displays

Measures of Central Tendency

The most familiar measure of central tendency is the mean, or average, but other measures can be more useful in certain situations.

Directions: Use the data set shown below to answer questions 1 through 5.

32	31	33	44	35
44	37	44	40	41
38	38	40	32	44

1. **Which of these is the mean of the data set?**

   A 44

   B 38.2

   C 35.8

   D 13

2. **Another data entry, 60, is added to this set. Which of these statements describes the value 39.6?**

   F It is the mean.

   G It is the range.

   H It is the mode.

   J It is the median.

3. **Which measure of central tendency is shared between the original set above and the set of values 25, 44, 32, 61, 28, 44, 37, 50, 39, 44, 25, 25, 37, 44?**

   A mean

   B median

   C mode

   D range

4. What is the median of the data set? Please enter your response in the grid.

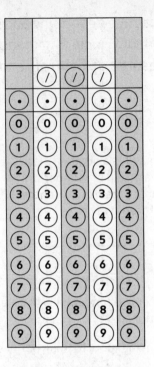

5. What is the range of the data set? Please enter your response in the grid.

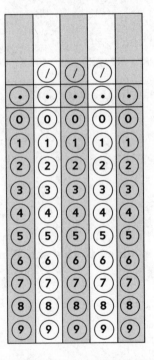

Directions: Answer the question below.

6. A data set has an even number of data items. When ordered from least to greatest, the middle two numbers are x and y. What expression describes the median of the data set?

F $x - y$

G $x + y$

H $\dfrac{x - y}{2}$

J $\dfrac{x + y}{2}$

Finding a Missing Data Item

Sometimes an average is a goal you want to meet, and you'll need to find a missing piece of data to see if you can achieve your goal.

Directions: Answer the questions below.

7 In a science class, Amy wants to earn an 84% or better. The grade for the class is an average of the four tests taken. On the first three tests, she scored a 78%, 82%, and 86%. What is the lowest percentage she can make on the fourth test and still meet her goal?

A 78%

B 80%

C 88%

D 90%

8. Dontell sells software for a computer company. If he sells a weekly average of at least $1,000 in new software over an 8-week period, he will receive a bonus. His weekly sales for the first 7 weeks are shown in this chart. How much does Dontell need to sell in Week 8 to receive the bonus?

Dontell's Weekly Sales	
Week	**Sales**
1	$900
2	$1,500
3	$785
4	$895
5	$973
6	$1,100
7	$875

F $715

G $785

H $972

J $7,028

9. Allison wants to earn a 90% in her history class. The grade for the class is an average of the grades on four tests. She earned an 87%, 85%, and 92% on three tests. Which equation can she use to find out whether her goal is achievable?

A $\dfrac{97 + 85 + 92 + 90}{3} = x$

B $\dfrac{87 + 85 + 92 + x}{4} = 90$

C $\dfrac{87 + 85 + 92 + x}{3} = 90$

D $\dfrac{87 + 85 + 92 + 90}{4} = x$

 Test-Taking Tip

When finding a missing data item, set up your equation correctly with the variable on the appropriate side. Then, correctly use order of operations to solve for the missing data item. Be sure to check that your answer makes sense in the context of the problem.

10. Wes wants to earn an 85% or better in his history class. The grade for the class is an average of the grades on six tests. On the first five tests, Wes scored 68%, 89%, 92%, 85%, and 80%. Which score on the last test will earn Wes at least an 85%?

F 85

G 90

H 92

J 96

11. Karina's office is open for 10 hours a day, Monday through Friday. She worked 4 hours on Monday, 6 hours on Tuesday, 8 hours on Wednesday, and 7 hours on Thursday. She plans to work on Friday. How many hours does Karina need to work on Friday in order to average exactly 7 hours per day for the entire week? Please enter your response in the grid.

Weighted Averages

In some situations, a grade or other piece of data counts more than others, so it's important to know how to find an average when items are not all worth the same weight.

Directions: Consider the frequency chart below that represents how many pairs of jeans a given number of shoppers at a mall own. Use the chart to answer questions 12 and 13.

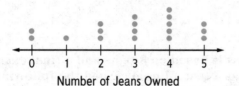

Number of Jeans Owned

12. Which is the mean number of jeans owned by those surveyed?

F 2

G 3

H 4

J 5

13. Suppose two more shoppers are surveyed. How many jeans would each need to own so that the average number of pairs of jeans owned was 2.75?

A 0 and 1

B 1 and 1

C 2 and 3

D 1 and 3

Directions: Answer the questions below.

14. Tanya is a photographer. She has 30-minute, 60-minute, and 90-minute sessions available. She charges $75 for a 30-minute session and has 25 booked this month. She charges $150 for a 60-minute session and has 30 booked this month. She charges $200 for a 90-minute session and has 15 booked this month. Which is the average price Tanya will charge for each session this month?

F $52.08

G $133.93

H $162.50

J $3,125.00

15. A bakery sells 30 cupcakes at $3 each, 12 cakes at $20 each, and 40 loaves of bread at $4 each. What is the average price of an item sold?

A $5.98

B $9.00

C $18.15

D $490

16. The final grade in Miguel's chemistry class is based on 3 tests and a final exam. The final exam is worth 3 times as much as a test. Miguel earned the following test grades: 87, 82, 94. He earned a 91 on the final exam. Which of these is Miguel's final grade in the class?

F 87.0

G 88.5

H 89.3

J 94.0

17. Shannon runs a business, selling 4 different types of products. After a month in business, she determines the following information.

Product	Percent of Total Sales	Profit Per Item
A	50%	$7
B	30%	$5
C	15%	$4
D	5%	$6

What is Shannon's average profit per item?

A $5.25

B $5.50

C $5.90

D $6.25

This lesson will help you practice understanding how to summarize information about different categories using bar graphs and circle graphs. Use it with Core Lesson 8.2 *Display Categorical Data* to reinforce and apply your knowledge.

Key Concept

Bar graphs and circle graphs are convenient ways of displaying data that fall into categories. Both types of graphs allow the viewer to see data at a glance. Bar graphs are appropriate to show the absolute size of various categories. Circle graphs show what percentage of the total is made up by the various categories.

Core Skills

- Interpret Data Displays
- Interpret Graphs

Bar Graphs

In a bar graph, the relative length of the bars shows the relative size of the different categories.

Directions: Use this bar graph for questions 1 and 2.

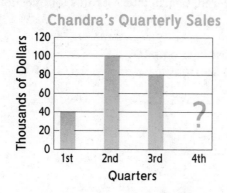

Chandra's Quarterly Sales

1. **What was the percent of increase of the second quarter over the first quarter?**

    A   60%

    B   100%

    C   150%

    D   200%

2. Chandra recorded her quarterly sales in a bar graph. Chandra will get a bonus of $5,000 if her average quarterly sales for the year reach $70,000. What must her sales be for the fourth quarter in order for Chandra to earn the bonus? Please enter your response in the grid.

Directions: Use this bar graph that shows the amount of interest paid on a $100,000 mortgage for two different payback periods and for three different yearly interest rates for questions 3 through 5.

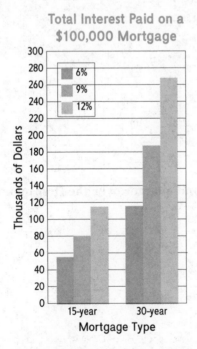

Total Interest Paid on a
$100,000 Mortgage

3. Suppose you want to borrow $100,000 to purchase a house, and the interest rate of your loan is 12%. Which of these is the estimate of the difference in total interest you would pay if you take out a 30-year loan instead of a 15-year loan.

A   about $75,000

B   about $150,000

C   about $200,000

D   about $250,000

Test-Taking Tip

Look carefully at any notations beside the vertical scale when reading a bar graph. If there is a notation reading "Thousands of Dollars," for instance, a reading on the scale that says "$100" is to be interpreted as $100,000.

4. Which of these is the estimated total amount of interest would you pay on a 30-year $100,000 mortgage at an interest rate of 9%?

    F   about $50,000

    G   about $80,000

    H   about $118,000

    J   about $190,000

5. Over the life of a 30-year mortgage at 6%, what is the average interest paid per year for a mortgage of $100,000? Round the average interest to the nearest $1,000. Please enter your response in the grid.

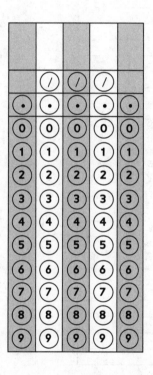

Directions: Answer the questions below.

6. You want to create a bar graph displaying data in a range from $0 to $1000. Which of these would be the best interval between lines on the vertical scale?

    F $5

    G $100

    H $500

    J $1,000

7. A transportation authority is analyzing the number of riders on its buses each month to determine how ridership changes during the height of tourist season. Which of these graphs would be *least* helpful to show the number of riders each month, in thousands?

Month	Riders
May	55,000
July	85,000
September	65,000
November	50,000

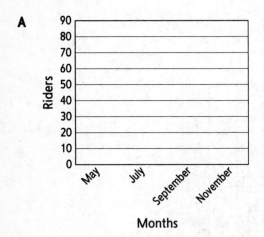

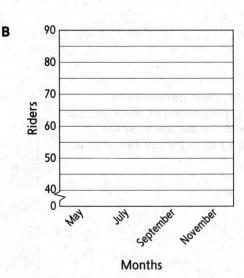

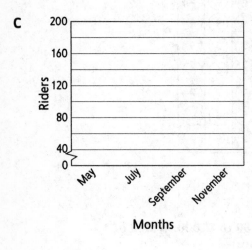

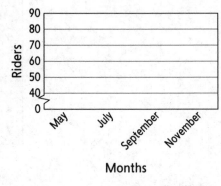

Circle Graphs

In a circle graph, the relative size of the wedges shows the relative size of the fractions of the whole represented by the different categories.

Directions: Use this circle graph that represents the election results for a mayoral race, for questions 8 through 12.

Mayoral Election Results 50,200 votes cast

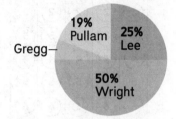

8. **What percent of the votes did Gregg receive? Please enter your response in the grid.**

9. Which candidate received about $\frac{1}{5}$ of the votes cast?

   A Gregg

   B Lee

   C Pullam

   D Wright

10. What percent of registered voters voted in this election?

   F more than 80%

   G between 30% and 60%

   H between 60% and 80%

   J Not enough information is given.

11. According to information provided by the graph, what number of votes did Lee receive? Please enter your response in the grid.

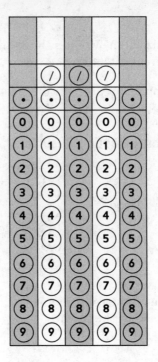

12. Wright received the votes of $\frac{1}{3}$ of the registered voters. Therefore, what portion of registered voters voted for Lee?

F $\frac{1}{12}$

G $\frac{1}{8}$

H $\frac{1}{6}$

J $\frac{1}{4}$

Directions: Answer the question below.

13. Consider this circle graph.

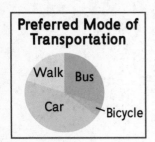

Preferred Mode of Transportation

Which is the second most popular mode of transportation?

A Bicycle

B Bus

C Car

D Walk

Welty Family Budget
(cents per $1.00)

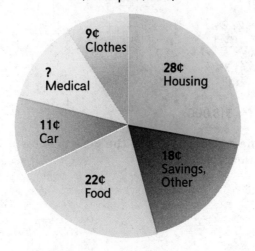

14. What is the approximate ratio of the amount the Weltys budget for housing to the amount they budget for clothes?

   F 1:3

   G 2:1

   H 1:2

   J 3:1

15. If the Weltys earn $3,875 each month, how much of this income will most likely be spent for food?

   A about $700

   B about $750

   C about $800

   D about $850

16. How much would the Weltys have to earn per month for their monthly housing budget to exceed their monthly food budget by $540?

   F $9,000

   G $90,000

   H $1,928.57

   J $2,454.54

Directions: Use these graphs for questions 17 through 19.

Mike's Bicycle Store
Percent of Total Profit, by Quarter

19.4%
2nd   22.2%
3rd
16.7%
1st   41.7%
4th

Total Profit = $18,000

17. The profit for Mike's Bicycle Store for the four quarters of the year is shown. What is the store's mean (average) profit per quarter?

   A $4,500

   B $5,600

   C $6,250

   D $6,800

18. Which expression tells the dollar amount of profit made during the first quarter?

   F $1.67 \times \$15,000$

   G $16.7 \times \$18,000$

   H $0.167 \times \$15,000$

   J $0.167 \times \$18,000$

19. After receiving some late payments, Mike's Bicycle Store finds it made more money in the 3rd quarter than the charts show. The 3rd quarter now accounts for 44% of the yearly total. To the nearest thousand, what was the total amount of late payment money?

   A $5,000

   B $6,000

   C $7,000

   D $8,000

Directions: Answer the question below.

20. In a circle graph reporting the answers to a poll asking whether a landfill operation should be approved in Westerley, the segment for the No votes is twice as large as the segment for the Yes votes, and the segment for Undecided respondents is one-third the size of the segment for the Yes votes. In all, 500 people were interviewed. How many were Undecided?

   F 50

   G 75

   H 100

This lesson will help you practice displaying data in different ways (dot plots, histograms, box plots) to highlight certain aspects of the data. Use it with Core Lesson 8.3 *Display One-Variable Data* to reinforce and apply your knowledge.

Key Concept

Dot plots, histograms, and box plots are different ways to display one-variable data, data in which only one quantity is measured. Each display highlights different characteristics of the data set.

Core Skills

- Interpreting Data Displays
- Model with Mathematics

Dot Plots

You can use a dot plot to find the mean, median, and mode of the data set.

Directions: Consider this information and dot plot to answer questions 1–5.

Cassie surveyed students in her class and asked how many computers are in each person's household.

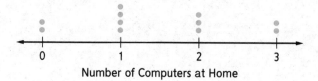

Number of Computers at Home

1. **What is the median number of computers in a household?**

    A 0

    B 1

    C 2

    D 3

2. **If Cassie surveys 55 people, how many people would she expect to have 3 computers?**

    F 2

    G 5

    H 10

    J 45

3. What fraction of students surveyed have at least 2 computers at home? Please enter your response in the grid.

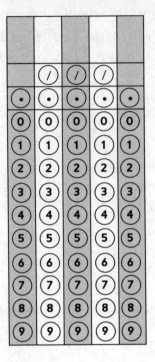

4. Which of these is the data set for this dot plot?

F 0, 1, 2, 3

G 0, 0, 1, 1, 1, 2, 2, 2, 2, 3, 3

H 0, 0, 1, 1, 1, 1, 2, 2, 2, 3, 3

J 0, 0, 1, 1, 1, 1, 2, 2, 3, 3, 3

5. Cassie surveyed an additional person and found that he had 3 computers at home. What is the mode of the new data set?

A 0

B 1

C 2

D 3

Histograms

While histograms look like bar graphs, they are different because the data is numerical instead of categorical.

Directions: Use this histogram to answer questions 6–10.

This histogram records the ages of first-time mothers at a local hospital.

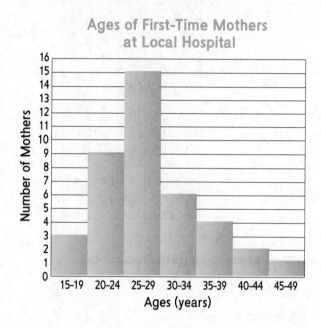

6. What is the range, in years, of each interval shown in the histogram?

   F 4

   G 5

   H 7

   J 15

7. How many of the first-time mothers are older than 34?

   A 1

   B 5

   C 7

   D 13

8. What percent of first-time mothers are younger than 30?

   F 27%

   G 32.5%

   H 55%

   J 67.5%

9. How many more first-time mothers were in their 20s than in their 30s? Please enter your response in the grid.

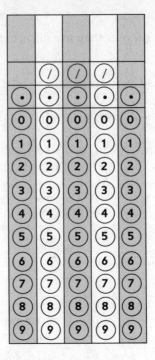

10. Which prediction for 120 first-time mothers at the hospital is incorrect?

    F There could be expected to be 6 between 40–44.

    G There will be a greater percent in their 20s than in their 30s.

    H There will be a greater percent in their teens than in their 40s.

    J There will be about 3 times more in the 15–19 range than in the 49–45 range.

 Test-Taking Tip

When interpreting a data display, remember that not all displays show the same information. Be sure to read labels carefully so that you can confirm what is actually conveyed in the data display. If the question requires listing a set of data, you can check your work by sketching a data display to see if it matches the one given in the problem.

Box Plots

A box plot can help you understand and visualize the clustering or spreading of a set of data.

Directions: Consider this box plot to answer questions 11–15.

Henry took a survey of his friends to find out how much money they make per hour, the results are shown in this box plot.

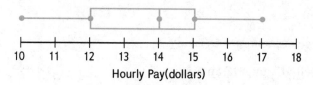

Hourly Pay(dollars)

11. What is the median hourly pay among Henry's friends?

A $10

B $12

C $14

D $17

12. What is the range of the data?

F 7

G 10

H 14

J 17

13. Raul's hourly pay is represented by the 1st quartile in the data set, and Caitlin's hourly pay is represented by the 3rd quartile. How many more dollars does Caitlin earn than Raul if they both work 10 hours? Please enter your response in the grid.

14. Which of these is a possible data set for this box plot?

F 10, 10, 11, 12, 14, 14, 14, 15, 16, 17, 17

G 10, 10, 11, 11, 12, 13, 13, 14, 15, 16, 17

H 10, 11, 12, 12, 13, 14, 14, 15, 16, 17, 17

J 10, 11, 12, 13, 13, 14, 14, 15, 15, 16, 17

15. Based on the box plot, which of these statements is true?

A Half of Henry's friends make between $15 and $17 an hour.

B Half of Henry's friends make between $12 and $15 an hour.

C One quarter of Henry's friends make between $14 and $17 an hour.

D One quarter of Henry's friends make between $10 and $14 an hour.

Directions: Answer the questions below.

16. A data set contains the following values.

25, 30, 40, 42, 9, 9, 12, 10, 15, 25, 36, 41, 45, 10, 12, 25, 26

Which list shows the five numbers that you would use to display this data set in a box plot?

F 9, 10, 15, 36, 45

G 9, 11, 25, 36, 45

H 9, 11, 25, 38, 45

J 9, 12, 26, 40, 45

17. Consider this data set, which shows the duration, in minutes, of Tonya's last several phone calls. The length of one call is unknown.

8, 13, 20, 14, 6, 12, x, 18, 4, 11, 16

In a box plot of the data set, the whiskers extend from 4 to 8 and from 16 to 20. Which of these could be the value of x?

A 4

B 10

C 17

D 21

This lesson will help you practice analyzing and displaying two-variable data using tables, scatter plots, and line graphs. Use it with Core Lesson 8.4 *Display Two-Variable Data* to reinforce and apply your knowledge.

Key Concept	Core Skills
Tables, scatter plots, and line graphs are all ways to show information that relates one thing to another, like temperature to time of day or height to weight. We call these displays of two-variable data, because there are two items.	• Build Lines of Reasoning • Interpret Graphs

Tables

Tables can organize and display a wide array of data including prices of items at a restaurant, sports statistics, and populations of cities.

Directions: Use this table to answer questions 1 and 2.

This table represents the number of ants, bacteria, and birds in an environmental setting.

	Week 1	Week 2	Week 3	Week 4
Ants	50	147	268	319
Bacteria	8	201	472	981
Birds	125	119	108	102

1. **How many more bacteria than birds were there during week 3?**

   A 117

   B 204

   C 209

   D 364

2. **Which week(s) had more bacteria than ants and birds combined?**

   F Week 2 only

   G Week 4 only

   H Weeks 3 and 4

   J Weeks 1 and 2

Directions: Use this information to answer questions 3 and 4.

At a restaurant, there are various prices for side dishes. Vegetables are priced at $1.29 for 1 side, $2.39 for 2 sides, and $3.19 for 3 sides. Potatoes are priced at $1.79 for 1 side, $2.99 for 2 sides, and $3.89 for 3 sides. Fruits are priced at $1.49 for 1 side, $2.89 for 2 sides, and $4.19 for 3 sides.

3. **Consider this table.**

	1 side	2 sides	3 sides
Vegetables			
Potatoes		*x*	
Fruits			

Which value should replace *x* in the table?

A $2.39

B $2.99

C $2.89

D $3.19

4. **Consider this table.**

	1 side	2 sides	3 sides
Vegetables			
Potatoes			
Fruits			*y*

Which value should replace *y* in the table?

F $2.89

G $3.19

H $3.89

J $4.19

Directions: Answer the question below.

5. A company makes tank tops, t-shirts, and long-sleeve shirts by four different designers. A table representing the data is being made such that the designers are shown in the columns of the table. How many rows should the table have? Please enter your response in the grid.

Directions: Use this table to answer questions 6–8.

This table below shows the amount of rainfall (in inches) for four cities during a five-month period.

	April	May	June	July	August
Smithville	8.3	4.7	7.7	6.2	4.8
Jonesville	5.7	6.3	2.4	3.8	1.7
Frankville	6.6	4.2	3.5	7.9	2.5
Robertville	9.4	7.7	6.4	8.8	9.2

6. Which city had the most rainfall in April and May combined?

F Frankville

G Jonesville

H Robertville

J Smithville

7. Which city had two consecutive months with the least amount of rain?

A Frankville

B Jonesville

C Robertville

D Smithville

8. What was the total amount of rainfall, in inches, for the city of Smithville over the five-month period? Please enter your response in the grid.

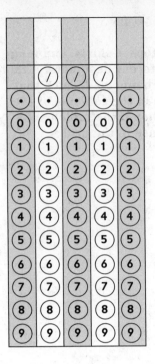

Scatter Plots

Scatter plots are used to plot distinct points relating two variables, whether or not a relationship may actually exist.

Directions: Answer the questions below.

9. Consider this scatter plot.

   Which table represents the data shown in the scatter plot?

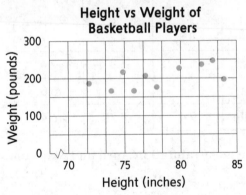

Height vs Weight of Basketball Players

A

Height (inches)	83	80	77	72	74	76	84	75	82	78
Weight (pounds)	250	230	210	190	170	170	200	220	240	180

B

Height (inches)	83	80	77	72	74	76	84	75	82	78
Weight (pounds)	250	175	210	150	170	170	200	200	240	180

C

Height (inches)	250	230	210	190	170	170	200	220	240	180
Weight (pounds)	83	80	77	72	74	76	84	75	82	78

D

Height (inches)	250	175	210	190	170	170	200	200	240	180
Weight (pounds)	83	80	77	72	74	76	84	75	82	78

Scatter plots do not represent functions with unique outputs for each input. If the x-value in the horizontal axis is in the data set more than once, there may be more than one y-value above it.

Directions: Use this scatter plot to answer questions 10 and 11.

This scatter plot shows earnings during a two-week period for a group of teenagers.

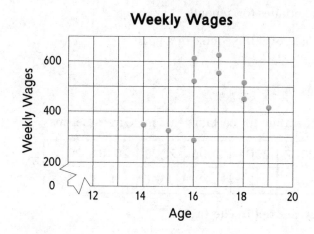

Weekly Wages

10. **What percent of teenagers made less than $450 during the two-week period?**

    F 30

    G 40

    H 50

    J 60

11. **What is the approximate combined earnings for the two 18-year-olds?**

    A $775

    B $875

    C $975

    D $1,075

Line Graphs

Line graphs are useful to display data that can increase or decrease at any time, such as company profits or the temperature outside.

Directions: Answer the question below.

12. Which of these would be <u>most</u> appropriate to display with a line graph?

    F   List prices of two brands of cars and trucks.

    G   Number of people in the neighborhood that have a pet.

    H   Amount spent for groceries, rent, and utilities for a month.

    J   Number of inches of rainfall each month over the course of a year.

Directions: Use this table to answer questions 13–17.

This table shows a city's average winter temperature for certain years in degrees Celsius.

Year	1998	2000	2002	2004	2006	2008	2010	2012
Temperature	8	6	4	12	9	5	1	7

13. Which line graph shows the data represented in the table?

A
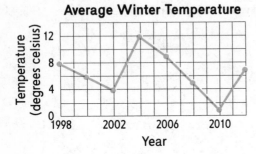

B
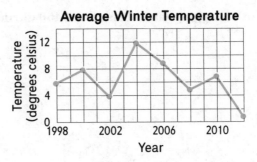

C
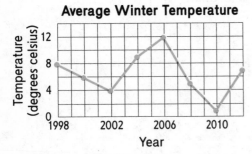

D
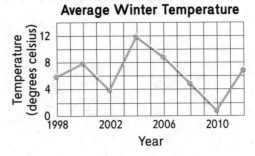

14. What is the trend that can be concluded from the graph?

    F   The average temperature increases every year.

    G   The average temperature decreases every year.

    H   There is no trend between year and temperature.

    J   There is an increase in temperature one year, and then a decrease the next year.

15. The sum of the average temperatures of which two years is equal to the average temperature of 2004?

A 2006 and 2012

B 2008 and 2012

C 2000 and 2002

D 2000 and 2008

16. Which year had the highest average temperature? Please enter your response in the grid.

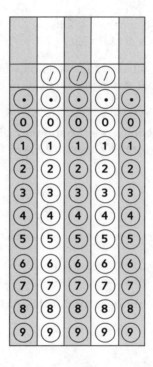

17. Which year had the lowest average temperature? Please enter your response in the grid.

Directions: Answer the questions below.

18. **Which scenario describes a situation where there may be a positive correlation between the two variables, but a change in one variable does not cause the change in the other variable.**

    F   A: number of minutes of exercise a week
        B: rate of heart disease

    G   A: number of hours studying for an exam
        B: scores on an exam

    H   A: daily intake of refined sugar, in grams
        B: number of cavities in a dental visit

    J   A: number of gallons of oil used to heat a home in a month
        B: number of mittens sold at a department store each month

19. **Consider this table that compares the number of hours of sunlight and the average daily temperature, in degrees Fahrenheit, over four months.**

Friday	Temp.
10.5	45
11.5	52
12.5	59
13.5	66

    What kind of function would best model this data?

    A   linear; positive slope

    B   linear; negative slope

    C   quadratic; positive end behavior

    D   quadratric; negative end behavior

20. **Which linear function best fits the data shown in the graph?**

    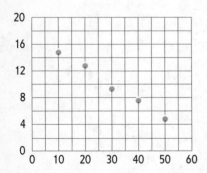

    F $y = -0.25x + 18$

    G $y = -2.5x + 18$

    H $y = 18x - 0.25$

    J $y = -18x + 2.5$

Lesson 1.1

Rational Numbers, p. 1

1. B   The numbers represented on the number line are the numbers -3, $\frac{1}{2}$, and 2.

2. J   The product of two integers is an integer. When rational numbers are multiplied, the numerators and denominators are multiplied together, which is a product of integers.

3. C   Rational numbers can be written as a ratio of two integers. Therefore, irrational numbers are numbers that cannot be written as the ratio of two integers.

4. G   The square root of 1 equals 1, which is a rational number.

Fractions and Decimals, p. 2

5. C   All of the numbers start with the number 2. The fractional portion of each number can be divided out to get the numbers $\frac{6}{10} = 0.6$, $\frac{3}{12} = 0.25$, $\frac{3}{4} = 0.75$, $\frac{3}{8} = 0.375$, and $\frac{6}{9} = 0.\overline{6}$, respectively. Therefore, the numbers, from least to greatest, are $2\frac{3}{12}$, $2\frac{3}{8}$, $2\frac{6}{10}$, $2\frac{6}{9}$, $2\frac{3}{4}$.

6.

All four numbers begin with 10. The next place value is the tenths place, which 5 is the largest of the other options.

7. A   The number 5 goes into 28 five times with 3 as a remainder.

8. H   The number 3 goes into 47 fifteen times with 2 as a remainder.

9. C   If all of the values are written as decimals, $7\frac{3}{8}$ would be written as 7.375, which is the smallest value of all the answer choices.

Absolute Value, p. 4

10. F   Moving left 3 units from the number 2 gives the value of -1. Moving 3 units right from the number 2 gives the value of 5.

11. D   The distance between -6 and 3 can be found by computing $|-6 - 3| = |-9| = 9$.

12. G   The sum of the expression $-17 + 8$ is -9. The absolute value equals 9.

13. C   The expression $217 - 538$ shows how many bags are left once the new orders came in. This is equal to -321, or that 321 bags are now on back order.

Lesson 1.2

Factors and Multiples, p. 5

1. **A** The unknown branch originates from the product 6, and the known factor is 3. So, the unknown factor is 2.

2. **H** The prime factors of 60 are 2, 2, 3, and 5. Written in the standard form for prime factorization, $60 = 2^2 \times 3 \times 5$.

3. **D** Each group needs the same number of distance runners and sprinters. The number of distance runners and sprinters in each group is a factor of the total distance runners (20) and sprinters (25). The GCF of 20 and 25 is 5. Therefore, $20 \div 5 = 4$, and $25 \div 5 = 5$, for a total of 9 runners per group.

4. **H** The LCM of 12 (buckles in a pack) and 16 (straps in a pack) is 48. Dividing the LCM by the number in each pack for each item, the craftsman should buy 4 packs of buckles and 3 packs of straps.

5. 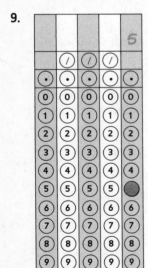 The GCF of the dimensions, 6, is the side length of the largest grid square the artist can make, so the area of the largest grid square is 36 square inches.

Properties of Numbers, p. 7

6. **F** The equation is an example of the Distributive Property: $2(6 + 3) = 2 \times 6 + 2 \times 3$.

7. **B** The Commutative Property of Addition allows you to change the order of addends: $x + y = y + x$.

8. **J** From the Properties of Addition, Vendor A sold the same amount of tee shirts as the total tee shirts sold by Vendor C and D together.

9. The equation shows a product equal to the sum of two products. A factor in the product on the left is the sum of two of the factors on the right. This is an example of the Distributive Property: $5 \times 35 = 5 \times (20 + 15) = 5 \times 20 + 5 \times 15$.

10. **F** The volume of a box is the product of its three dimensions. When the height is tripled and the length is multiplied by one-third, a factor of $3 \times \frac{1}{3} = 1$ is multiplied to the volume. This will keep the volume unchanged.

Order of Operations, p. 9

11.

When $m = 7$, the expression inside the parentheses simplifies to 0. Division by 0 is undefined, so the expression is undefined as well.

12. H Using the order of operations, the only expression shown that simplifies to a value greater than 70 is $100 - \dfrac{5}{2} \times 10 = 75$.

13. C The error was in evaluating exponents before performing operations in parentheses; according to the order of operations, parentheses should be simplified before all other operations.

14. F The shirts cost (3×15) dollars, the jacket costs $(30 - 5)$ dollars, and she subtracted 10 dollars off her cost by using the gift card. So, her total purchase was $(3 \times 15 + (30 - 5)) - 10$ dollars.

15. B From the order of operations: $5 + \dfrac{(6^2 - 10)}{2} + 3$; $5 + \dfrac{(36 - 10)}{2} + 3$; $5 + \dfrac{26}{2} + 3$; $5 + 13 + 3 = 21$

16. H The order of operations starts with simplifying within parentheses, moving left to right following the next steps of the order of operations. Inside the parentheses, the next step that can be simplified using the order of operations is multiplication/division, of which $\dfrac{36}{9}$ is the left-most example.

Lesson 1.3

Exponential Notation, p. 11

1. B The expression 14^2 gives the area of the room in square feet. The installation cost is the sum of the cost for the tile and the installation fee. So, the total cost of the installation is given by the expression $2.50 \times 14^2 + 175$.

2

Substituting $x = 4$ and $y = 2$ into the expression gives $x^2 + y^3 = 4^2 + 2^3$. Evaluating according to the order of operations, the expression has a value of $16 + 8 = 24$.

3. C The amount for each sod purchase can be found by calculating the cost per square foot times the area covered. Of the choices shown, the most expensive choice is purchasing sod from Shop C to cover an area of 18 feet by 18 feet: $\$0.60 \times 18^2 = \$194.40$.

4. F The 6 large containers have a total volume of 6×4^3, and the small container has a volume of 3^3. The total volume of dirt that is needed to fill all the containers is the sum of these values: $6 \times 4^3 + 3^3$.

5.

The equation is true when $y^a = 1$, as $13 + 1 = 14$. Since we are told that this is true for all y, it must be that $a = 0$ by the rules of exponents.

Rules of Exponents, p. 13

6. G When an exponent is located inside and outside of a set of parentheses, you can apply the Power of a Power Property to simplify the expression.

7. B According to the Power of a Power Property, $m \times 4 = -12$. So, $m = -3$.

8. J Use the Product of Powers Property and the Quotient of Powers Property to find the value of each expression. Of the choices shown, $12^{-3} \times 12^4 = 12$ has the least value.

9. D Apply the Power of a Power Property: $(2^2 \times 3^3)^4 = 2^8 \times 3^{12}$.

Scientific Notation, p. 14

10. H A number written in scientific notation is the product of a number greater than or equal to 1 and less than 10, and a power of 10. The number Olivia wrote, 65.2, is a number greater than 10. Moving the decimal in 65.2 to the left one place will produce a valid first factor and will also increase the power of 10 by 1.

11. B A number written in scientific notation is the product of a number greater than or equal to 1 and less than 10, and a power of 10. The decimal point in 0.0000000504 is moved 8 places to the right to form the first factor, 5.04, so the power of 10 factor must be 10^{-8}.

12. J The number of bacteria in one Petri dish (645,300,000) can be written as 6.453×10^8. Since the biologist uses 10 Petri dishes, multiply this number by 10 to get 6.453×10^9.

13. C The value of 4.2×10^5 is 420,000, and the value of 6.7×10^3 is 6,700. Adding $420,000 + 6,700$ gives 426,700, which is written in scientific notation as 4.267×10^5.

Lesson 1.4

Square Roots and Cube Roots, p. 15

1. C $4^4 = 256 \rightarrow \sqrt[4]{256} = 4$

2. F The old plates had an area of 25π in^2 and the new plates need to be 50% larger, so $\pi r^2 = 37.5\pi$. Solve for r; $r \approx 6.12$. Now double r to find the diameter; $d = 12.2$ in.

3. A The cube root of a negative integer is larger than the original integer; for example, $\sqrt[3]{-27} = -3$ and $-3 > -27$.

4. H The area of a square is $A = s^2$. Substituting $A = 350$, solve for s; $350 = s^2$, $s = \sqrt{350} \approx 18.7$ ft.

5. B Set up a proportion: $\dfrac{1\ \text{ft}^3}{7.48\ \text{gal}} = \dfrac{V\ \text{ft}^3}{10,000\ \text{gal}}$. Therefore, $V = \dfrac{10,000}{7.48}\ \text{ft}^3$, so the side length must be $\sqrt[3]{\dfrac{10,000}{7.48}} \approx 11$ ft.

6. J If a positive integer is not a perfect square, its square root is an irrational number.

7.

The fence has a side length of $\sqrt{56.25}$ ft. Multiply $s = 7.4$ by 4 to find the total perimeter.

8.

$\sqrt[3]{4,000} \approx 15.87$ ft

9. A The first block has a volume of 1 ft^3. For the second block to be twice as heavy, it needs a volume of 2 ft^3, so its side length will be $\sqrt[3]{2}$ ft.

Radicals and Rational Exponents, p. 17

10. H The speed of the fly is $\sqrt{2}$ m/min. The perimeter of the window is 4 m, so the fly will need $\dfrac{4}{\sqrt{2}} \approx 2.8$ minutes to walk around it.

11. D $\sqrt[3]{9^2} = \sqrt[3]{81} \approx 4.33$

12. F Since the volume is 750, one side length is $\sqrt[3]{750}$ and therefore the area is $\left(\sqrt[3]{750}\right)^2 = \left(750^{\frac{1}{3}}\right)^2 = 750^{\frac{2}{3}}$.

13. D $\dfrac{\sqrt{96}}{\sqrt{12}} = \sqrt{8} = \sqrt{4 \cdot 2} = 2\sqrt{2}$.

14. G Since the area is 800, one side length is $\sqrt{800}$. Therefore the volume is $\left(\sqrt{800}\right)^3 \approx 22,627$ in^3.

15. D Since negative integers do not have square roots, the value of x would have to be nonnegative.

16.

$$\frac{\sqrt[3]{108}(\sqrt[3]{16})}{\sqrt{9}} = \frac{\sqrt[3]{27}(\sqrt[3]{4})(\sqrt[3]{16})}{\sqrt{9}} = \frac{\sqrt[3]{27}(\sqrt[3]{64})}{\sqrt{9}} = \frac{3(4)}{3} = 4$$

17. A The rules for the root of a root are similar to the rules for the power of a power;
$$\sqrt{\sqrt[6]{2}} = \sqrt{2^{\frac{1}{6}}} = \left(2^{\frac{1}{6}}\right)^{\frac{1}{2}} = 2^{\frac{1}{12}} = \sqrt[12]{2}.$$

18. F $\sqrt{40} = 2\sqrt{10}$, and the parentheses mean to multiply. The other parts are the same as what appears in the original expression.

19. B Terms with unequal exponents and unequal root values cannot be divided without being separately evaluated first.

20. H Of the choices, only $\sqrt{48}$ is less than 7 so it is the least.

21.

$$\frac{\sqrt[3]{54}(\sqrt[3]{4})}{\sqrt{125}(\sqrt{5})} = \frac{\sqrt[3]{9 \cdot 6 \cdot 4}}{\sqrt{25 \cdot 5 \cdot 5}} = \frac{\sqrt[3]{27 \cdot 8}}{\sqrt{25 \cdot 25}} = \frac{3 \cdot 2}{25} = \frac{6}{25}$$

Lesson 2.1

Ratios, p. 21

1. B The ratio of boys to girls is $\frac{500}{120}$. Dividing the numerator and denominator by 20 gives the equivalent ratio $\frac{25}{6}$.

2. J You want to buy $7 + 5 = 12$ pounds of screws at \$3.48 per pound, so the cost will be
$12 \times \$3.48 = \$41.76$.

3. C Pigs:Cows and Chickens:Horses are each less than 1, so neither can be the greatest if other ratios are greater than 1. Cows:Chickens equals $\frac{3}{2}$, making that ratio greater than Horses:Pigs, which equals $\frac{4}{3}$.

4. G The first car travels at $\frac{240}{4} = 60$ miles per hour; the second car travels at $\frac{275}{5} = 55$ miles per hour. The difference is 5 miles per hour.

5.

The unit price of a tablet in the medium bottle is $\frac{\$7.80}{100} = \$0.078$. The unit price of a tablet in the large bottle is $\frac{\$11.70}{150} = \$0.078$. The difference is 0.

[Grid-in answer: 0]

6. H The ratio "a to b" can also be written as $a{:}b$ and $\frac{a}{b}$.

7. D The unit price of the rolls in the 4-pack is $\frac{\$6.36}{4 \text{ rolls}} = \frac{\$1.59}{1 \text{ roll}}$. This is $0.30 less than the cost of a single roll.

Proportions, p. 23

8. G The rate Megan worked is $\frac{\$48}{5 \text{ h}}$. If she works at the same rate, then $\frac{\$t}{3 \text{ h}}$ will be an equivalent rate, so the correct proportion is $\frac{48}{5} = \frac{t}{3}$. Solve this proportion to find $t = \$28.80$.

9. C The company makes screws at the rate of $\frac{500 \text{ screws}}{4 \text{ sec}}$. The number of screws made in 1 minute (60 seconds) will have the same proportion, so $\frac{500}{4} = \frac{n}{60}$. Solve this proportion to find $n = 7,500$.

10.

The gallons of paint needed per square foot is $\frac{2 \text{ gal}}{800 \text{ ft}^2}$. Painting the whole room will require a proportional amount, so $\frac{2}{800} = \frac{x}{1,800}$. Solve this proportion to find $x = 4.5$.

[Grid-in answer: 4.5]

11. **A** The caloric content of the candy is $\frac{240 \text{ calories}}{1.2 \text{ oz}}$. Solve the proportion $\frac{240}{1.2} = \frac{x}{4}$ to find the calories in a 4-oz bar, and then subtract 240 to find the difference.

12.

The amount of whole-wheat flour used, x, can be found using the proportion $\frac{5}{2} = \frac{x}{1\frac{1}{3}}$. The number of cups remaining is $4 - x$.

2 / 3

Scale, p. 25

13.

The scale of the map is $\frac{1 \text{ in.}}{15 \text{ mi}}$. Because the scale is constant, $\frac{1}{15} = \frac{2.5}{x}$. Solve this proportion to find $x = 37.5$.

37.5

14. **G** The ratio of Jessica's height to her shadow is $\frac{5.5 \text{ ft}}{8 \text{ ft}}$. The same ratio will apply to the tree, so $\frac{5.5}{8} = \frac{h}{14}$, where h is the height of the tree. Solve this proportion to find $h = 9.625$.

15. **D** The scale is $\frac{1 \text{ in.}}{48 \text{ ft}}$, so $\frac{1}{48} = \frac{6.4}{s}$, where s is the height of the side. Solve this proportion to find $s = 307.2$.

16. **H** The ratio of the side length of the neighbor's pentagon, s, to the side length of Mike's pentagon, 8, is $\frac{3}{2}$, so $\frac{s}{8} = \frac{3}{2}$ and $s = 12$. Therefore, the perimeter of the neighbor's pentagonal garden is $5 \times 12 = 60$.

17.

The scale factor is $\frac{19 \text{ ft}}{0.5 \text{ ft}} = 38$.

18. G   The greatest dimension, 50 feet, limits the scale factor. Therefore, the largest scale factor that will allow the scale model to fit on the base is 20 inches:50 feet which reduces to 2 inches:5 feet.

19. A   Each leg is triple the length of the base, and the base is 10 inches. So each leg is $3 \times 10 = 30$ inches.

Lesson 2.2

Percent of a Number, p. 27

1. D   Divide 23 by 25 because 23 is the part and 25 is the whole; $\frac{23}{15} = 0.92 = 92\%$.

2. H   Calculate $100 - 24 = 76$ to find the percentage of runners who prefer to run wearing shoes. Then multiply $0.76 \times 300 = 228$.

3. D   Multiply $3,000 \times 0.79 = 2,370$.

4. G   Susan correctly calculated $28 \div (4 + 6) = 2.8$, but this is not the correct way to find the percent of students who chose pink or red as their favorite color. You must find the number of students who chose pink or red, divide by the total number of students, and then multiply by 100.

5. B   You must first find the number of students who chose pink or red and then divide by the total number of students. Choice B shows the total number of students divided by the number of students who chose pink or red, so it is not correct.

6.

Nine out of twenty squares are shaded, so to find the percentage, calculate $9 \div 20 = 0.45$. Then multiply $0.45 \times 100 = 45\%$. The equivalent fraction with a denominator of 100 is $\frac{45}{100}$.

Percent Change, p. 29

7. C $(126 - 180) \div 180 = -0.30$, so the discount is 30%. Remember that percent change can be positive or negative, but discounts are always expressed as positive percents.

8. G The amount of the discount is $54.99 \times 0.2 \approx \$11.00$, so the sale price is $\$54.99 - \$11.00 = \$43.99$. To find the profit per sweater, subtract the cost to manufacture the sweater from the price: $\$43.99 - \$20.00 = \$23.99$. Then multiply $\$23.99 \times 200 = \$4,798.00$, so the company makes a profit of about $4,800.00.

9. C To find the amount saved, multiply the original price by the discount as a decimal: $43 \times 0.05 = \$2.15$, $12 \times 0.3 = \$3.60$, $36 \times 0.15 = \$5.40$, and $25 \times 0.2 = \$5.00$.

10. H Ron calculated $\frac{159}{212} \times 100$. To calculate percent change, you subtract the original amount from the new amount, then divide by the original amount, and then multiply by 100.

11. C The correct calculation is $\frac{159 - 212}{212} \times 100 = -25$, so the discount is 25%. Remember that percent change can be positive or negative, but discounts are always expressed as positive percents.

12.

To calculate percent change, subtract the old membership fee from the new membership fee, divide by the old membership fee, and then multiply by 100. The percent change was about −14% for Year 2, about 4% for Year 3, 20% for Year 4, about −7% for Year 5, and about 4% for Year 6.

Simple Interest, p. 31

13. D To find simple interest, use the formula $I = Prt$. Using this formula, Bank A pays $240 in simple interest, Bank B pays $250, Bank C pays $252, and Bank D pays $280.

14. J To find simple interest, use the formula $I = Prt$, where $P = 10,000$, $r = 0.0299$, and $t = 4.5$: $10,000 \times 0.0299 \times 4.5 = \$1,345.50$. Then add this amount to the original amount: $\$10,000.00 + \$1,345.50 = \$11,345.50$.

15.

The total amount of interest that would be paid to Bank A is $20,000 \times 0.042 \times 10 = \$8,400$. Because the time for Bank B is 15 years, the student would pay $\$8,400 \div 15 = \$560.00$ in interest per year to Bank B. To find the interest rate as a percent, calculate what percent 560 is of 20,000: $\frac{560}{20,000} \times 100 = 2.8\%$.

16. J The table shows that Chad pays \$90 in interest each month, so the interest is paid monthly. Divide the amount of interest per month by the cost of the car to find the percent: $90 \div 5{,}000 = 0.018$ and $0.018 \times 100 = 1.8\%$.

17. C Chad pays \$90 per month, and there are 12 months in a year: $12 \times 90 = 1{,}080$.

18. J The amount of interest earned each year is $0.05 \times 1{,}000 = \$50.00$. To find the number of years it will take to earn \$1,000 in interest, divide: $1{,}000 \div 50 = 20$.

Lesson 2.3

Factorials, p. 33

1.

$5! = 5 \times 4 \times 3 \times 2 \times 1 = 120$

2. J The total number of ordered arrangements of 6 people is 6!.

3.

Find the product of the individual possibilities; $3 \times 3 \times 2 = 18$.

4. J The possible outcomes are $2 \times 52 \times 4 = 416$.

Answer Key

5. $2^3 > 3!$ but $2^4 < 4!$

6. G $3 \times 4 \times 9 \times 6 = 648 < 1,000$

7. The factors of 105 are 3, 5, and 7. Tops are the largest factor.

8. The difference between 6! and 5! is 600 because $6! = 720$ and $5! = 120$; $720 - 120 = 600$.

Permutations, p. 36

9. A Since $P(n, k) = \dfrac{n!}{(n-k)!}$ by definition, then $P(7, 3) = \dfrac{7!}{(7-3)!}$.

10. G $5! = 5 \cdot 4 \cdot 3 \cdot 2 \cdot 1 = 120$

11. B   The number of possible combinations is $9 \times 8 \times 7 = 504$. Set up a proportion to find the time; $\dfrac{1 \text{ set}}{5 \text{ sec}} = \dfrac{504 \text{ sets}}{x \text{ sec}}$.
Therefore, $x = 5(504) = 2{,}520$ seconds. To change 2,520 seconds to minutes, divide it by 60; 42 min.

12. H   The number of possible castings is $8 \times 7 \times 6$.

13. B   There are 3 choices for the first man, 2 for the second, and 1 for the third. The same is true for the women. So, $3 \times 2 \times 1 \times 3 \times 2 \times 1 = 36$ different ordered arrangements.

14. H   To solve this problem, you need to find a pair of factors for 380 that differ by 1; $20 \times 19 = 380$. Therefore, the total number of members is 20.

15. C   To solve this problem, you need to find three consecutive numbers whose product is $210 = 7 \times 6 \times 5$. Therefore there are 7 comedians.

Combinations, p. 37

16. G   Combinations do not have any particular order and ice cream toppings do not have to have any particular order. The other situations need order and are therefore permutations.

17. A   There are 3 ways to have one topping; $3(\$6.95) = \$20.85$. There are 3 ways to have two toppings; $3(\$7.95) = \$23.85$. And, there is 1 way to have three toppings; $1(\$8.95)$. The sum of these costs is the total cost; $\$20.85 + \$23.85 + \$8.95 = \$53.65$.

18. F   The number of different bouquets is $\dfrac{7 \times 6 \times 5 \times 4 \times 3}{5!}$.

19. D   The order of friends does not matter, so Keena should have found the number of combinations, which is 10.

20. G   The first prize can be chosen 8 different ways, leaving 7 different ways to choose the second prize. The 2 honorable mentions is then a combination of 2 out of 6; $\dfrac{6 \times 5}{2!}$. Therefore the total number of ways to choose is $8 \cdot 7 \cdot C(6, 2) = 56 \cdot \dfrac{6 \cdot 5}{2} = 840$.

Lesson 2.4

Probability of Simple Events, p. 39

1. B   Janine's family has 3 members and there are a total of 390 people attending, so $\dfrac{3}{390}$ can be simplified to $\dfrac{1}{130}$.

2. J   The complement of an event is all other possible events. The probability of the event (drawing a red marble), and its complement (drawing a blue, yellow, or green marble) have a sum of $1 \left(\dfrac{1}{4} + \dfrac{3}{4} = 1 \right)$.

3. C   Rolling a number cube has 6 possible outcomes and 3 of these are even. Therefore, the probability of rolling an even number is 3 out of 6, or $\dfrac{1}{2}$.

4. G   The tree diagram shows the six different possible uniform combinations. A uniform that has a green shirt and black pants is one of the six possibilities; therefore, the probability is $\dfrac{1}{6}$.

5. B   Since 28 is more than half of 50, there are more possibilities that are less than 28. Therefore, there is a greater likelihood that Sal's guess is too high.

6.

The best prediction for the number of red covers sold is $\dfrac{40}{100}$ or 40%. Since the table shows the last 25 cell phone cover purchases, the answer will be 40% of 25 or 10 red covers.

Probability of Compound Events, p. 41

7. A Probability of spinning a red section is $\frac{2}{6} = \frac{1}{3}$. Spinning a red section twice has a probability of $\frac{1}{3} \times \frac{1}{3} = \frac{1}{9}$.

8. F The probability that Aaron draws a white marble on the first draw is $\frac{4}{9}$. The probability that Aaron draws a white marble on the second draw is $\frac{3}{8}$ (the first marble was not replaced). The probability of drawing white marbles on both draws is $\frac{4}{9} \times \frac{3}{8} = \frac{12}{72} = \frac{1}{6}$.

9. D Since rolling a number cube has 6 possible outcomes (1, 2, 3, 4, 5 or 6), rolling it 30 times means each number is likely to be rolled exactly 5 times ($5 \cdot 6 = 30$).

10. F The probability of Allen choosing a king is $\frac{1}{4}$. The probability of flipping a head is $\frac{1}{2}$. The probability of first choosing a king and then flipping a head is $\frac{1}{4} \times \frac{1}{2} = \frac{1}{8}$.

11. C The probability of choosing a queen on the first draw is $\frac{2}{4}$. The probability of choosing a queen on the second draw is $\frac{1}{3}$ (the first queen is removed). The probability of choosing a queen, setting it aside, and then choosing another queen is $\frac{2}{4} \times \frac{1}{3} = \frac{2}{12} = \frac{1}{6}$.

12. F The probability of drawing a vowel on the first try is $\frac{6}{26}$. The probability of drawing a vowel on the second try is $\frac{5}{25}$. The probability of drawing a vowel twice is $\frac{6}{26} \cdot \frac{5}{25} = \frac{30}{650} = \frac{3}{65}$.

Lesson 3.1

Algebraic Expressions, p. 43

1. C The total cost for renting the wedding hall can be determined by adding the fee for the wedding hall, 350, plus the cost per person for food, $10p$, plus the cost per person for beverages, $4p$; $350 + 10p + 4p$.

2. F The airplane starts at 35,000 feet then descends to the ground, which indicates subtraction. The rate of descent is 10 feet per second which can be represented by $10t$; $35{,}000 - 10t$.

3. B The perimeter of the garden can be calculated by multiplying the width and the length each by 2, then adding the products. In this case the width is w and the length is $(4w - 5)$. Therefore, the perimeter can be represented by $2w + 2(4w - 5)$ or $2(4w - 5) + 2w$.

4. J Robert's earnings in one week equal his regular earnings, $12.00 times 40 hours, plus his overtime pay, 1.5 times $12.00 times hours of overtime; $12(40) + 12(1.5)h$.

5. 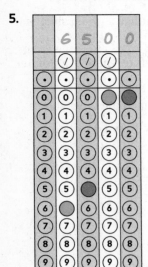 After being driven off the lot, the truck is worth $17,000; $20{,}000 - 3{,}000$. There are 60 months in a five-year period and since the truck depreciates $175 per month, the total depreciation equals $10,500 ($175 times 60). The value of the truck after five years is $17,000 − 10,500, which equals $6,500.

6. H Cole cuts the pizza into 12 equal slices and removes n slices; $12 - n$. The number of remaining slices, $12 - n$, he then divides by 5; $\dfrac{(12 - n)}{5}$.

Linear Expressions, p. 45

7. A To simplify the expression, first distribute the coefficient 2, then rearrange the expression so that like terms are next to each other. Last, combine like terms; $7x - 8 + 2x - 10 = 7x + 2x - 8 - 10 = 9x - 18$.

8. H The coefficient 1 is distributed through the first set of parentheses and the coefficient -4 through the second set; $-3x + 10 - 4x + 12$.

9.

The missing term is the constant term so the coefficients outside the parentheses only need to be distributed to the constant terms and then find the sum; $2(3) + 5(7) = 6 + 35 = 41$.

10. F To simplify, distribute the coefficient -5 through the parentheses; $-5(-3x + 2) = 15x - 10$.

11.

It is enough to consider only the constants because the sum of the constants in the original expression must be 25. Therefore, $-2(7) - 3(-5) + a(6) = -14 + 15 + 6a = 1 + 6a$, which gives $1 + 6a = 25$ and therefore, $a = 4$.

12. H When a coefficient of a parentheses expression is not written, the coefficient is actually 1. To remove the subtraction in front of the second parentheses, a -1 must be distributed through the parentheses and therefore the constant term would be -1. So, $-20 - 1 = -21$ not -19.

13. A The original expression is simplified as: $(4x - 17) + (-8x + 9) - 2(x - 14) = 4x - 17 - 8x + 9 - 2x + 28 = 4x - 8x - 2x - 17 + 9 + 28 = -6x + 20$. Changing the coefficient of $(x - 14)$ to positive 2 would only change the distribution product of the last x term and the last constant term. Therefore, the step before the final simplification would instead be $4x - 8x + 2x - 17 + 9 - 28 = -2x - 36$.

Evaluating Linear Expressions, p. 47

14.

Substitute $y = 2$ into the expression, then simplify; $3 + \frac{3}{2}(2) = 3 + 3 = 6$.

15. A Substitute $x = 5$ and $y = -3$ into each expression and simplify. The greatest value is $2(5) - 3(-3) = 10 + 9 = 19$.

16. G Substitute $x = -2$ and $y = 4$ into each expression and simplify; $2(-2) + 4 = -4 + 4 = 0$.

17. C Substitute $a = 3$ and $c = 5$ into the expression and simplify; $18(3) + 7(5) = 54 + 35 = \$89$.

18. H To determine who will earn the most, substitute 6 for m and 10,000 for s in each expression. Then simplify. Lorena will earn the most, $3,500(6) + 0.45(10,000) = \$25,500$.

19. C Company A's charge for using 3 GB equals $\$25.00 + \$2.00(3) = \$31.00$. Company B's charge for using 3 GB equals $\$20.00 + \$3.00(3) = \$29.00$. The difference is $\$31.00 - \$29.00 = \$2.00$.

20. J The cost for each company per year is: Take Your Trash charges $\$60.00(4) = \$240$, Dump Brothers charge $\$30.00(12) = \$360.00$, and Garbage Removal charges $\$50.00(6) = \$300.00$.

Lesson 3.2

One-Step Equations, p. 49

1. B The phrase "a number tripled" corresponds to the expression "$3n$". Set $3n$ equal to 72 and solve for n by dividing both sides by 3.

2. J The phrase "8 less than x" corresponds to the expression "$x - 8$." Set $x - 8$ equal to 31 and solve for x by adding 8 to both sides.

3. A The total number of people (150) divided by the number of players on each team (s) will represent the number of teams (10); $150 \div s = 10$. Solving for s gives $s = 150 \div 10 = 15$.

4. G Let n represent the total amount earned on Thursday. The landscaper needs to subtract what he paid for gas, $\$18$, from n and set that expression equal to $\$90$.

5.

The grid shows: **4 0**

Let p represent the number of pots sold. The amount Ginger made is $45p$. Set $45p$ equal to $1,800 and solve for p by dividing both sides by 45.

6. G Divide both sides of the equation by -12 to find the solution.

Multi-Step Equations, p. 51

7. C The number 5 is being added to a product, $4z$, to get 49. To solve, subtract 5 from both sides and then divide both sides by 4.

8. F Substitute 101 for j and solve for b by subtracting 3 from both sides and then dividing both sides by 2.

9.

The grid shows: **3 6**

To solve, distribute 8 through the parentheses, then subtract 128 from both sides, and then divide both sides by 8 to find the value of m. Then multiply that value by 9.

10. F The phrase "the difference of a number and 5" corresponds to the expression "$x - 5$". Multiply that expression by -9 and set equal to 81: $-9(x - 5) = 81$. To solve, distribute -9 through the parentheses, then add 45 to both sides, and then divide both sides by -9.

11. C Let b represent the cost of each lunch. Keondre spends $b + \$2$ each visit. So, $3(b + \$2)$ is the total amount he spent that month, which is equal to $39. Now solve for b.

12.

To solve, subtract 27 from both sides and then divide both sides by -6.

13. B To solve, first combine like terms; $-3n - 9n = -12n$. Now, subtract 30 from both sides and then divide both sides by -12.

Lesson 3.3

Inequalities, p. 53

1. B Translate the inequality into words; the solution to the inequality is all numbers less than or equal to -4. There should be a solid circle at -4 and the arrow should go left.

2. J The number of boys currently registered, 71, and the number of boys left to be registered, b, must be more than 312. This translates to $b + 71 > 312$.

3. C The phrase "three times the sum of a number and seven" translates to $3(x + 7)$ and "half of the number" translates to $\frac{1}{2}x$. Use this to write the inequality, making sure the correct sign is used.

4. J The circle at 300 should be open and the arrow should go right.

One-Step Inequalities, p. 54

5. D To solve the inequality, divide both sides by -3. When dividing by a negative number, the inequality sign must be reversed. So the solution is $x > -\frac{8}{3}$. And $-\frac{8}{3}$ is not the same as $-\frac{3}{8}$.

6. F Subtracting 12 from both sides of the inequality simplifies to $x < -3$. Choose the correct graph that represents the inequality.

7. A Substitute -8 into each of the inequalities to see which inequality is not true after simplifying; $4(-8) \geq -24$; $-32 \geq -24$.

8. G Multiply both sides of the inequality by -7 to solve the inequality, making sure to reverse the inequality sign.

9. D Using p as the profit needed to meet your goal, the inequality that represents the situation is $p - 400 \geq 1,000$. Add 400 to both sides of the inequality to solve. Then choose the correct graph that models the situation.

10.

The grid shows the answer **70**.

Since Carden has never scored more than 30% of the team's points, then $21 \leq 0.3p$ represents the situation. Divide both sides by 0.3 to solve the inequality.

Multi-Step Inequalities, p. 56

11.

The grid shows the answer **16**.

The inequality that represents this situation is $7.75p - 10 \leq 120$. Adding 10 to both sides and then dividing both sides by 7.75 results in $p \leq 16.774194$. Therefore, the group can't buy more than 16 pizzas.

12. H   Simplifying both the left and right sides of the inequality results in $-2t - 10 > 6t - 16$. Adding $2t$ and 16 to both sides of the inequality results in $6 > 8t$. Divide both sides by 8, reduce the fraction, and choose the correct graph.

13. D   To find the average of the five tests, first add all five scores with x being one of the scores because it is the unknown score of the test yet to be taken. Then divide that sum by 5. That expression must be greater than or equal to 85. Therefore, the inequality is $\dfrac{91 + 74 + 83 + 86 + x}{5} \geq 85$.

Lesson 3.4

Expressions and Equations, p. 57

1.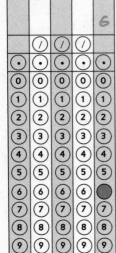
The expression 4 + 0.25(8) can be used to determine the cost of the ride: 4 + 2 = $6.00.

2. **F** Let n represent the number of lawns Freddy mows. Therefore, $25n$ is the amount of money that Freddy earns. Set this equal to the $110 that he needs to earn minus the amount of money he has already saved: $25n = 110 - 35$.

3. **B** To set up an equation use the formula, rate · time = distance. In this case, the distance is 165 miles and the rate is s. The time is equal to 3.25 hours minus 0.25 hours (15 minutes = $\frac{1}{4}$ of an hour = 0.25 hours). Therefore, the equation is $s(3.25 - 0.25) = 165$, or $165 = s(3.25 - 0.25)$.

4. **G** Julie begins with $150 then pays $8 per hour for cleaning. The amount she pays $8h$ is subtracted from her beginning cash of $150 ($150 - 8h$). The amount she has left is the difference or $54.

5. **D** Juan begins by warming up for 5 minutes. This is then added to the amount of time he spends running, which is 12 minutes per mile ($12m$). Then 10 minutes is added for the amount of time he spends cooling down. The expression is $5 + 12m + 10$.

6. **F** Bailey's interest is $540 = \$2{,}000(r)(9)$, so $r = 3\%$. Curt's interest is $540 = \$2{,}700(.04)(t)$, so $t = 5$.

7.
The delivery fee will not affect her savings because it is added on at the end and she will pay it under both scenarios. So, the expression, $940(1.06) = \$996.40$ is how much Marcella will pay this week for the treadmill. The expression $[940(0.90)](1.06) = \$896.76$ is next week's sale price with tax. Marcella will save $99.64.

8. **H** The cost of 4 pounds of apples is 4(2). The cost of three pounds of pears is $3p$. The total cost is given by the equation, $4(2) + 3p = 15.50$, which can be used to determine the cost of pears per pound.

Inequalities, p. 60

9. **A** The inequality $1{,}000 - 7f \geq 300$ can be used to determine how much carpet he can buy. To solve, subtract 1,000 from both sides, $-7f \geq -700$. Now divide both sides by -7, $f \leq 100$. Since division by a negative occurred, the inequality sign was reversed.

10. **J** The inequality $m \leq 16(32)$ can be used to solve this problem. Therefore, $m \leq 512$ miles.

11. **C** Miguel's rate is $\dfrac{360 \text{ miles}}{18 \text{ days}} = 20$ miles per day. The inequality representing the goal for the number of miles is $500 \leq 360 + 20x$, where x is the number of additional days riding 20 miles each day. Subtracting 360 from both side and then dividing by 20 gives the inequality $7 \leq x$.

12. **J** To solve $5 - 2x \leq 35$, subtract 5 from both sides, $-2x \leq 30$, then divide by -2 and flip the symbol since division by a negative occurred, $x \geq -15$.

13. **A** The amount of money that Tara is spending can be represented by the expression $15 + 8p$. Since Tara has \$60 to spend, her expenses must be less than or equal to \$60. The inequality $15 + 8p \leq 60$ represents this situation. It can be rewritten as $60 \geq 15 + 8p$. Subtracting $8p$ from both sides, $60 - 8p \geq 15$.

14. **H** The amount of money that Jake makes can be represented by the expression $85 + 30x$. The inequality $85 + 30x \geq 500$ would be used to determine how many hours Jake must work to earn at least \$500.

15. **D** In order to ride a roller coaster, a person's height must be at least 54 inches. This means that the height can actually be 54 inches or greater than 54 inches.

16. **H** Jolene can spend less than or equal to \$110.

17. **C** The three options for salary are $32{,}000 + 0.1s$, $25{,}000 + 0.12s$, or $50{,}000$, where s is the sales amount. The first time that all the salary options are greater than \$50,000 is when $s = \$225{,}000$. At that time, the \$32,000 option is the greatest amount.

18. The expression $230 + 4d$ represents how much money Maddie will spend if she spends d dollars per week and \$230 for the boots when she returns. She can spend at most \$450 total, which is represented by the inequality $230 + 4d \leq 450$. Subtract 230 from both sides and then divide both sides by 4; $d \leq \$55$.

Lesson 4.1

Identifying Polynomials, p. 63

1. **B** A binomial has two terms.

2. 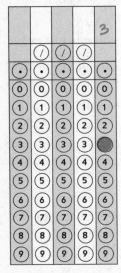 The degree of the term with the greatest degree is the degree of the polynomial.

3. **C** Standard form for a polynomial has the terms written, left to right, in descending order according to their degree.

4. **G** In a polynomial, variables must have whole-number exponents. Variables may not appear in denominators. A constant c divided by $-9x^2 + 7x$ has two powers of x in the denominator; $\dfrac{-1}{9x^2 + 7x}$.

5. **B** To simplify, combine like terms; $-6x^2 - 7x^2 - 2x + 8x + 10 - 8 = -13x^2 + 6x + 2$.

6. Since the degree of the product is 3 and the binomial $(x - 2)$ has degree 1, the degree of B must be 2.

Evaluating Polynomials, p. 65

7. **A** Miles evaluated $(-2)^2$ as -4, but $(-2)^2 = 4$.

8.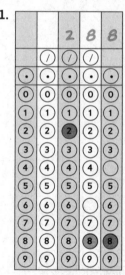

Substitute 3 for x and simplify, following the correct order of operations; $\frac{1}{2}(3)^3 + \frac{3}{4}(3) - 7 = \frac{27}{2} + \frac{9}{4} - 7 = \frac{35}{4}$.

9. A Substitute 2 for t and simplify, following the correct order of operations: $-16(2)^2 + 38(2) + 5 = -16(4) + 76 + 5 = -64 + 76 + 5 = 17$.

10. H Substitute 4 for x in the expressions for the length and the width of the rectangle. Then multiply the length by the width to determine the area; $(5(4) - 1)(5 + 2(4)) = (20 - 1)(5 + 8) = (19)(13) = 247$.

11.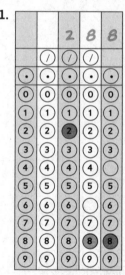

Substitute $x = 20$ into the expressions for the length and the width of the rectangle. Then add the lengths of all four sides; $(5(20) - 1) + (5 + 2(20)) + (5(20) - 1) + (5 + 2(20)) = 99 + 45 + 99 + 45 = 288$.

Operations with Polynomials, p. 67

12. H Simplify $(5 + 2x)(5x - 1)$ by using the Distributive Property and combining like terms; $25x - 5 + 10x^2 - 2x = 10x^2 + 23x - 5$.

13. C Simplify $2(5x - 1) + 2(5 + 2x)$ by using the Distributive Property and combining like terms; $10x - 2 + 10 + 4x = 14x + 8$

14. J Apply the Distributive Property and combine like terms; $2x^3 - x^2 + 3x - 4x^2 + 2x - 6 = 2x^3 - 5x^2 + 5x - 6$

15. C To find the opposite of a polynomial, reverse the sign of each term.

16. G Find the expression for the area of the triangle multiplied by 10 and then simplify; $\frac{1}{2}(2x + 4)(x - 1)10 = \frac{1}{2}(2x^2 + 2x - 4)10 = (x^2 + x - 2)10 = 10x^2 + 10x - 20$

17. B Find the expression for the perimeter of the rectangle and then simplify; $2(9x - 1) + 2(3x + 5) = 18x - 2 + 6x + 10 = 24x + 8$.

Lesson 4.2

Factoring Out Monomials, p. 69

1. **D** Use prime factorization for each term to determine the greatest common factor for the trinomial.

$30x^4y^4 = 2 \cdot 3 \cdot 5 \cdot x \cdot x \cdot x \cdot x \cdot y \cdot y \cdot y \cdot y$

$45x^2y^3 = 3 \cdot 3 \cdot 5 \cdot x \cdot x \cdot y \cdot y \cdot y$

$75xy^2 = 3 \cdot 5 \cdot 5 \cdot x \cdot y \cdot y$

Common numerical factors: 3, 5

Common variables: x, y, y

GCF $= 3 \cdot 5 \cdot x \cdot y \cdot y = 15xy^2$

2. **J** Factor out the greatest common factor, $15xy^2$, from each term. You can divide each term by the GCF to find the missing factors. $\dfrac{30x^4y^4}{15xy^2} = 2x3y^2$; $\dfrac{45x^2y^3}{15xy^2} = 3xy$; $\dfrac{75xy^2}{15xy^2} = 5$. Factored form is $15xy^2(2x^3y^2 + 3xy + 5)$.

3. **B** The coefficient of a monomial is the number in front of the variables.

4. **J** Factor out the greatest common factor, $9ab$, from each term. You can divide each term by the GCF to find the missing factors: $\dfrac{9ab^2}{9ab} = b$; $\dfrac{18a^2b}{9ab} = 2a$. Factored form is $9ab(b + 2a)$.

5. **C** Factor out the greatest common factor, 16, from each term. You can divide each term by the GCF to find the missing factors. Factored form is $16(x - 5)$.

6.

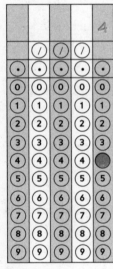

The greatest common factor of 8, 24, and 12 is 4.

7. **D** Factor out the greatest common factor, y^2, from each term. Then, divide each term by the GCF; $y^2(2x - 5 - 10xy)$.

Factoring Quadratic Expressions, p. 71

8. **H** To factor $x^2 - 8x + 7$, think of two numbers whose product is 7 and whose sum is -8; $(-1)(-7) = 7$ and $-1 + (-7) = -8$. Therefore, factors are $(x - 7)$ and $(x - 1)$.

9.

The quadratic expression is factored as $(x + b)(x + c)$ where $bc = -24$ and $b + c = -a$. The largest factor of -24 is 24, so using the factored expression $(x + -24)(x + 1) = x^2 - 23x - 24$ gives the largest possible value of 23 for a.

10. H $4x^2 - 4x - 24$ has a GCG of 4. Therefore, $4x^2 - 4x - 24 = 4(x^2 - x - 6)$. Since $(-3)(2) = -6$ and $(-3) + 2 = -1$, $x^2 - x - 6 = (x - 3)(x + 2)$. Therefore, $4x^2 - 4x - 24 = 4(x - 3)(x + 2)$.

11. D $12x^3 + 2x^2 - 10x$ has a GCG of $2x$. Therefore, $12x^3 + 2x^2 - 10x = 2x(6x^2 + x - 5)$. And $6x^2 + x - 5$ can be factored as $(6x - 5)(x + 1)$. Therefore, $12x^3 + 2x^2 - 10x = 2x(6x - 5)(x + 1)$.

12. F To factor $6x^2 + 13x - 5$, list all possible factors of 6 and -5, then substitute a set from each into the factored form and test until one combination works.
<u>Possible Factors:</u>
  6: $-1, -6$ and $-2, -3$ and 1, 6 and 2, 3
  -5: $-1, 5$ and 1, -5
The factored form will be in the form $(\quad x + \quad)(\quad x - \quad)$, since a and b are positive values and c is a negative value. The correct factorization is $(3x - 1)(2x + 5)$.

13. C $8x^3 + 2x^2 - 3x$ has a GCF of x. Therefore, $8x^3 + 2x^2 - 3x = x(8x^2 + 2x - 3)$. And, $8x^2 + 2x - 3$ can be factored as $(4x + 3)(2x - 1)$. Therefore, $8x^3 + 2x^2 - 3x = x(4x + 3)(2x - 1)$.

14. G $(x + 6)(x + 7) = (x^2 + 13x + 42)$

15. D $-16t^2 - 16t + 96$ has a GCF of -16. The student used the wrong signs in factoring the trinomial. The correct factorization is $-16(t + 3)(t - 2)$.

Lesson 4.3

Solving a Quadratic Equation by Factoring, p. 73

1. B The maximum height of the ball corresponds to the vertex of the graph. The maximum height cannot be negative in this context and should not be unreasonably high. The reasonable given value in feet is 50 feet.

2. J Given the quadratic equation $y = (x - c)(x - d)$, the two zeros of the graph are $x = c$ and $x = d$. In the context, the ball lands at the zero with the greater x value.

3. B The zero-product principle says that if the product of two quantities is zero $[(x - 4)(x + 5) = 0]$, then one of the quantities must equal zero $[x - 4 = 0$ or $x + 5 = 0]$. So, solve each equation for x.

4. H Since the situation calls for the product of the two integers, multiply x and $(x + 1)$ and set equal to 72, $x(x + 1) = 72$. Therefore, $x^2 + x - 72 = 0$.

5.

The quadratic factors into $(x-11)(x-12)$. The solutions are therefore, 11 and 12. The sum is then 23.

6. H Rewrite the equation $x^2 = 24 - 2x$ so that it is set equal to zero. Then factor, and use the zero-product principle to solve for x.

7. C Only the factors $(3x + 4)(2x - 3)$ multiply to get the expression $6x^2 - x - 12$.

Completing the Square, p. 75

8. J To determine the value of c, take half of 14 and square it.

9. B When completing the square, be sure to balance each side of the equation. Stanley only added 4 to the left side and not the right side also.

10. G Since the ball has dropped 36 feet when it hits the ground, substitute $d = 36$ in the equation $d = 16t^2$, and solve for t.

11.

Subtract the two equations: $18x = 288$. Solve to get $x = 16$.

12. J A quadratic equation will have no real solution if the solution is the square root of a negative number: $x = \pm\sqrt{-49}$.

13. A Begin by setting $3x^2 + 2x - 1 = 0$. Since the discriminant is a perfect square, 16, it is factorable.
Factor: $(x + 1)(3x - 1) = 0$. So, $x = -1$ or $\frac{1}{3}$. The smaller number is -1.

14.

Find the discriminant: $5^2 - 4(3)(-10) = 25 + 120 = 145$. Since the discriminant is positive, the equation has 2 real solutions.

15. A Before you determine the values for a, b, and c, set the equation equal to zero. Now $a = -4$, $b = 5$, and $c = -6$.

16. H Substitute $d = 240$ in the equation $d = \frac{x^2}{20} + x$, then solve for x using the quadratic formula where $a = \frac{1}{10}$,

$b = 1$, and $c = -240$: $x = \dfrac{-(1)\pm\sqrt{(1)^2 - 4\left(\frac{1}{20}\right)(-240)}}{2\left(\frac{1}{20}\right)} = \dfrac{-1\pm\sqrt{1 + 48}}{\frac{1}{10}} = \dfrac{-1\pm\sqrt{49}}{\frac{1}{10}} = \dfrac{-1 \pm 7}{\frac{1}{10}} = 60$ or -80.

17. B First set the equation equal to zero. Then determine that $a = 2$, $b = 5$, and $c = -4$. Now use the quadratic formula.

18. J Make the following substitutions into the quadratic equation: $a = 3$, $b = 8$, and $c = -3$ and simplify.

19. D The height of the object when it lands on the ground is $h = 0$. Use the quadratic formula on the equation $0 = -16h^2 + 16t + 5$ in order to solve for t.

Lesson 4.4

Simplifying Rational Expressions, p. 79

1. B Ratio of two polynomials; a constant over a polynomial of degree 1.

2.

Set the denominator unequal to zero to find the restricted value: $-x + 4 \neq 0$; $x \neq 4$.

3. C Set $x^3 - 9x = 0$ since a rational expression's denominator is undefined when it is 0.
Factor: $x(x^2 - 9) = x(x - 3)(x + 3)$. Set each equation equal to 0 and $x \neq -3, 0, 3$.

4. F   Set $x^2 - 4 = 0$ and factor $(x - 2)(x + 2) = 0$. So $x \neq -2, 2$. Then $\dfrac{x(x^2 - 4)}{x^2 - 4} = x$.

5. B   The rational expression is factored correctly. However, the expression is not defined when $x = -3$, since $(-3 + 3) = 0$. Therefore, when the term $(x + 3)$ is cancelled, the restricted value of $x = -3$ must be identified.

6. J   To simplify the expression, use the properties of exponents on each factor. For example, $\dfrac{(x - a)^{-3}}{(x - a)^{-4}} = $ $(x - a)^{-3-(-4)} = (x - a)^1$ by property of exponents. In order for the expression to be a rational expression, all factors with negative exponents must be moved from the numerator to the denominator or from the denominator to the numerator.

Multiplying and Dividing Rational Expressions, p. 81

7. C   Factor and simplify each rational expression first; cross out like terms that divided equal 1.

8. F   The expression can be rewritten as $\dfrac{(x + 4)(x - 2)}{2x(x + 4)} \cdot \dfrac{(x + 4)(x - 3)}{x(x - 3)}$. Setting the denominators equal to zero gives as the restricted values. Cancelling out like factors in the numerator and denominator leaves $\dfrac{x^2 + 2x - 8}{2x^2}$.

9.

Factor the first numerator and change to multiplication by taking the reciprocal of the divisor. Then there are two factors that cancel. $\dfrac{(x^2 + 4x + 3)(x - 3)}{(x + 4)(x - 3)} \cdot \dfrac{(x - 2)(x + 2)}{x^2 + 4x + 3}$.

The zeros of the factors give the restricted values of $x \neq -1, -3, 3, -4$ and the expression reduces to $\dfrac{x^2 + ax - 4}{x + 4} = \dfrac{x^2 - 4}{x + 4}$, so $a = 0$.

10. G   The product of the two side lengths is $\dfrac{2x}{(x^2 - 4)} \times \dfrac{(x^2 + 4x + 4)}{x^3} = \dfrac{2x}{(x + 2)(x - 2)} \times \dfrac{(x + 2)^2}{x^3} = \dfrac{2(x + 2)}{x^2(x - 2)} = \dfrac{2x + 4}{x^3 - 2x^2}$.

11. C   Sum is wrong because it means to add. It should be product.

12. G   The volume of the pool can be written as $V = L \times W \times H$. Substituting in the expressions given and dividing, the expression to find the height of the pool is $H = \dfrac{V}{L \times W} = \dfrac{\dfrac{(x + 4)(x - 1)}{x(x + 2)}}{\left(\dfrac{(x + 4)^2(x - 1)}{(x + 1)(x - 2)}\right) \times \left(\dfrac{(x - 2)^2(x + 1)}{x^2(x + 4)(x - 3)}\right)} =$

$\dfrac{(x + 4)(x - 1)}{x(x + 2)} \times \dfrac{(x + 1)(x - 2)}{(x + 4)^2(x - 1)} \times \dfrac{x^2(x + 4)(x - 3)}{(x - 2)^2(x + 1)} = \dfrac{(x + 4)^2(x - 1)(x + 1)(x - 2)x^2(x - 3)}{x(x + 2)(x + 4)^2(x - 1)(x - 2)^2(x + 1)} =$

$\dfrac{x(x - 3)}{(x + 2)(x - 2)}$.

Adding and Subtracting Rational Expressions, p. 83

13. B $\dfrac{1}{x} + \dfrac{1}{2x} = \dfrac{3}{2x}$

14.

Distance of the Rapids is $\dfrac{\text{time (hours)} \times 1 \text{ trip}}{2(\text{hours})}$;

Distance of The Bayou is $\dfrac{\text{time (hours)} \times 1 \text{ trip}}{(2 \times 2)(\text{hours})}$.

When they meet, the sum of the distance they each have traveled is the total trip or 1.

So $\dfrac{t}{2} + \dfrac{t}{4} = 1$. $t \approx 1.3$ hours

15. B Volume divided by depth equals the area of the top or bottom of the pool. There are two areas so you have to add them to get the total amount of paint needed. The area of the bottom of the first pool

is $\dfrac{x^3 + 12x^2 + 20x}{x + 2} = \dfrac{x(x + 2)(x + 10)}{x + 2} = x^2 + 10x$. The area of the bottom of the second pool is

$\dfrac{2x^3 + 7x^2 + 3x}{2x + 1} = \dfrac{x(x + 3)(2x + 1)}{2x + 1} = x^2 + 3x$. The total area for the two pools is $2x^2 + 13x$.

16. G $\dfrac{1}{2}$ is not a restricted value for x.

17. A $x = 1$ is a restricted value because of Sean's time to build the house.

Lesson 5.1

Points and Lines in the Coordinate Plane, p. 85

1. B Points whose x-coordinates are negative and whose y-coordinates are positive are in Quadrant II.

2. H All points on the line have y-coordinate -1.

3. C If a point is on the line $y = -x$, then its x- and y-coordinates will be opposites.

4. J All of the points in table J satisfy the equation $y = -x + 2$: $3 = -(-1) + 2$; $2 = -0 + 2$; $1 = -1 + 2$.

The Slope of a Line, p. 86

5. A This is the graph that has a slope equal to $\dfrac{1}{2}$ and crosses the y-axis at a negative value. The other answer choices have a negative slope or cross the y-axis at a positive value.

6. H Helen used the points $(-2, -4)$ and $(-1, -2)$ in the slope formula. However, she did not subtract the coordinates in the same order in the numerator and in the denominator. The correct calculation is $\dfrac{(-4 + 2)}{(-2 + 1)} = \dfrac{-2}{-1} = 2$.

7. B Two points on the line in graph B are $(-4, -1)$ and $(0, 2)$. Substituting into the slope formula gives $\dfrac{-1 - 2}{-4 - 0} = \dfrac{-3}{-4} = \dfrac{3}{4} = 0.75$.

8. F A line with positive slope rises from left to right, so the y-values are increasing.

9.

| | | 1 | / | 7 |

Use any two points and substitute into the slope formula: $\frac{2-1}{13-6} = \frac{1}{7}$.

10. J   The slope formula between two points is $m = \frac{y_2 - y_1}{x_2 - x_1}$. Using the first two ordered pairs, the slope calculation
is $\frac{1-0}{6.5-0} = \frac{1}{6.5} = \frac{10}{65} = \frac{2}{13}$.

Slope as a Unit Rate, p. 89

11. C   The graph with the greatest or steepest slope represents the Web site that charges the most.

12. H   The slope of the line in the graph is 25, so Painter A charges $25.00 per hour. The coefficient of x in the
equation $y = 35x$ is the slope, so Painter B charges $35.00 per hour.

13.

| | 1 | 2 | . | 5 |

After 2.5 hours, Rower A traveled $10(2.5) = 25$ miles. The table shows that Rower B was
traveling 15 miles per hour, so after 2.5 hours, Rower B traveled $15(2.5) = 37.5$ miles.
$37.5 - 25 = 12.5$.

14. H   The slope represents the unit rate. Substitute any two points in the table into the slope formula:
$\frac{300 - 150}{6 - 3} = \frac{150}{3} = 50$.

15. A   The slope represents the unit rate. The graph contains the points $(0, 0)$ and $(2, 6)$. Substitute these points into
the slope formula: $\frac{6-0}{2-0} = \frac{6}{2} = 3$. The unit rate is $3.00 per item.

16. J   In Graph A, each unit on the y-axis represents 20. In Graph B, each unit on the y-axis represents 10. The
graphs do not have the same slope and therefore, do not have the same unit rate either.

17.

Grid answer: 0 . 8 3

The slope is the unit cost for one printer cartridge. Use any two points in the table to find the unit cost at Store A: $\frac{100-50}{8-4} = \frac{50}{4} = 12.50$. Use any two points on the graph to find the unit cost at Store B: $\frac{35-0}{3-0} = \frac{35}{3} \approx 11.67$. $12.50 - 11.67 = 0.83$.

Lesson 5.2

Using Slope and y-Intercept, p. 93

1. **C** The standard form of a linear equation is $Ax + By = C$, and the definition states that A must be a whole number.

2. **J** Slope-intercept form is $y = mx + b$, where m is the slope and b is the y-intercept.

3. **B** Substitute the given values into slope-intercept form: $4 = 3(2) + b$. Solve this equation to find $b = -2$. Use the values of m and b to write the equation.

4. **J** The slope m is the cost per video and the y-intercept b is the one-time membership fee. The cost to rent 3 videos is \$1.00 per video plus the membership fee: $8 = 1(3) + b$; solve to find $b = 5$. Use the values of m and b to write the equation.

5. **A** The slope m is the cost per pound and the y-intercept b is the one-time membership fee. Use the values of m and b to write the equation.

6.

Grid answer: 9

Substitute the given values into slope-intercept form: $1 = 4(-2) + b$. Solve this equation to find $b = 9$.

7. **C** Point-slope form is $y - y_1 = m(x - x_1)$, where m is the slope and (x_1, y_1) is a point on the line.

8. **G** Point-slope form is $y - y_1 = m(x - x_1)$, where m is the slope and (x_1, y_1) is a point on the line.

Using Two Distinct Points, p. 95

9. C Two points on the line are $(0, 3)$ and $(2, 0)$. Use these points to find that $m = -\frac{3}{2}$. Because $(0, 3)$ is on the line, $b = 3$. Use the values of m and b to write the equation $y = -\frac{3}{2}x + 3$. Then rewrite this equation in standard form.

10. G Use the two points to find that $m = -2$. Choose either point and substitute its coordinates and $m = -2$ into point-slope form. Then write the equation in slope-intercept form by solving for y.

11. Use the points $(2, 18)$ and $(4, 26)$ to find that $m = 4$. Choose either of these points and substitute its coordinates and $m = 4$ into point-slope form. Simplify the equation and find the value of y when $x = 7$.

Using Tables, p. 96

12. H Each month, the total earnings will increase by the monthly salary. So you can add \$2,550 to \$12,650 to find total earnings for month 4.

13. D Use the table to identify any two points. Use these points to find the slope, and substitute the slope and the coordinates of any point from the table into point-slope form to find the equation. Substitute $x = 8$ into the equation to find that $y = \$79.00$, which is not more than \$80.00.

14. F The points $(-4, 0)$, $(0, -3)$, and $(4, -6)$ are all on the line.

15. D Use the table to identify any two points. Use these points to find the slope, and substitute the slope and the coordinates of any point in the table into point-slope form. Then write in slope-intercept form by solving for y.

16. Use the table to identify any two points. Use these points to find that $m = \frac{1}{4}$. The table shows that $(0, -1)$ is on the line, so $b = -1$. Substitute m and b into slope-intercept form to write the equation $y = \frac{1}{4}x - 1$. Substitute 1 for y and solve for x to find $x = 8$.

17. B $(1, 10)$ represents 1 mile in 10 minutes, and this ordered pair is not in the table.

Lesson 5.3

Using Ordered Pairs, p. 99

1. **B**   Substitute the values for x and y into the equation to find the correct table: $12(0) - (-4) = 4$, $12(1) - (8) = 4$, $12(2) - (20) = 4$. Therefore, B is correct.

2. **F**   Substitute each of the ordered pairs into the equation to determine which one does not work; $1 \neq 2(1)$.

3. **D**   The line and the table both contain the same ordered pairs: $(0,1)$, $(1, 4)$, $(2, 7)$.

4.

Substitute $x = -4$ into the equation and solve for y: $y = -2(-4) - 3$; $y = 8 - 3$; $y = 5$.
Substitute $y = -11$ into the equation and solve for x: $-11 = -2x - 3$; $-8 = -2x$; $x = 4$.

5. **D**   The ordered pair $(3, 4)$ is above the line. This ordered pair is different from the ordered pair $(4, 3)$, which is on the line.

6. **H**   The x-axis time is in 15-minute intervals, and the y-axis is total distance in miles. The points $(0,0)$ and $(60, 8)$ should be on the line.

7. **C**   The pattern is that $\frac{2}{15}$ of every x-value is the y-value and $\frac{2}{15}(120) \neq 12$.

Using Slope-Intercept Form, p. 102

8. **J**   A constant rate of $2 per album makes this scenario linear.

9.

The third graph has a negative slope and positive y-axis. The line passes through $(0, 2)$ and $(1, 0)$, so it has a slope of -2.

10. **J**   Moving down 2 units is -2 and then moving to the left 1 unit is -1. A negative divided by a negative makes the slope positive and therefore his graph represents a slope of 2 and not -2.

11. C   Two lines will either intersect at one point, never intersect, or intersect everywhere. These two lines intersect at the point $(0, 0)$ so they have the same x- and y-intercepts. However, Gina's line includes the point $(1, 100)$ while her friend's line includes the point $(1, 90)$ and therefore they don't intersect everywhere and Gina's slope is greater than her friend's slope.

12. H   Graph A shows total distance so at 40 minutes you are not 20 miles from home, you drove a total of 20 miles. Graph B lets you know that work is only 15 miles away. So you are actually 5 miles closer to your home with only 10 more miles to go.

13. D   The slope of the decreasing portion of the graph is $-\frac{1}{2}$. It includes the point $(30, 15)$, so the y-intercept is $y = 30$. Therefore the equation is $y = -\frac{1}{2}x + 30$.

14. J   Since Ted returned t-shirts and got money back as the number of days increased, the total amount he paid for all the t-shirts decreased. Therefore, as x increased, y decreased giving a decreasing slope.

15. B   The slope of the original graph is the speed of the runner, or 5 miles per hour. The slope of the new equation is $5 - 1 = 4$ and the y-intercept is the distance from the starting line. Therefore the equation is $y = 4x + 7$.

16. G   The y-intercept is the initial temperature, 37. The temperature is decreasing by 1 degree each 15 minutes or 4 degrees an hour. Therefore the equation is $y = -4x + 37$.

Lesson 5.4

The Graphing Method, p. 105

1. C   The solution is the point where the two lines intersect; $(-2, 10)$ is the solution to the system.

2. J   To write the system of equations, each equation would equal y the total cost. Then, the cost per mile is multiplied by the total miles x, and the fee is added. Therefore, the equation for Tow-a-Way is $y = 1.25x + 25$ and Haul-Ur-Car is $y = 1.50x + 15$.

3. C   Since $(5, 1)$ is the solution of the system, substitute this point into the second equation and solve for a; $a(5) - 5(1) = 15$, so $a = 4$.

4. G   To write the system of equations, each equation would equal y the total cost. Then, the cost per pound is multiplied by the total pounds x, and the cost of the container is added. Therefore, the equation for The Gummy is $y = x + 1.25$ and The Bear is $y = 2x + 0.5$.

5. A   To graph a system of linear equations, points for the graph must be determined. For the equation $y = x + 1.25$, points on the line include $(0, 1.25)$ and $(2, 3.25)$. For the equation $2x + 0.5$, points on the line include $(0, 0.5)$ and $(2, 4.5)$. The point where the two lines meet is $(0.75, 2)$ and is the solution to the system.

The Substitution Method, p. 107

6. F   A system of equations has no solution when the two lines have the same slope but different y-intercepts. Solve each equation for y: $4x + by = 5$ becomes $y = \frac{4}{b}x + \frac{5}{b}$ which has a slope $-\frac{4}{b}$ and y-intercept $\frac{5}{b}$; $2x + y = 3$ becomes $y = -2x + 3$ which has a slope -2 and y-intercept 3. If the slopes are equal, then $-\frac{4}{b} = -2$ and $b = 2$. The y-intercepts are different when $b = 2$ since $\frac{5}{b}$ becomes $\frac{5}{2}$ for the first equation and for the second equation $b = 3$.

7. D   Since $y = 0$, substitute this into either equation and solve for x; $x - 4(0) = 1, x = 1$.

8.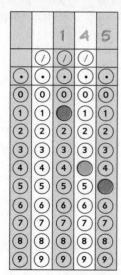

To write the system of equations, each equation would equal y the total amount saved. Then, the amount saved each week is multiplied by the number of weeks x, and the starting amount is added. Therefore, the equation for Diana is $y = 4.50x + 100$ and Megan is $y = 12.50x + 20$. To solve the system $y = 4.50x + 100$ and $y = 12.50x + 20$, the first equation can be substituted into the second equation for y and solved for x; $4.5x + 100 = 12.5x + 20$, $80 = 8x$, $x = 10$. Now $x = 10$ can be substituted into either equation and solve for y; $y = 4.5(10) + 100$, $y = 145$. The solution to the system is $145.

9. C   The number of containers sold by Water for You is decreasing from 12,500. The number of containers from Drink Up is increasing from 8,000. The month when they sell the same amount of containers, the number of containers will be between 8,000 and 12,500.

10.

To write the system of equations, each equation would equal y the number of containers. Then, the amount gained or lost is multiplied by the number of months x, and the initial amount is added. Therefore, the equation for Water for You is $y = -50x + 12,500$ and Drink Up is $y = 40x + 8,000$. To solve the system the first equation can be substituted into the second equation for y and solved for x; $-50x + 12,500 = 40x + 8,000$, $4,500 = 90x$, $x = 50$ months.

11.

To solve the system for the number of containers of water, the number of months (50) can be substituted into either equation and solve for y; $y = 50(50) + 8,000$, $y = 10,500$ containers.

12. J To write the system of equations, each equation would equal y the total cost to go to the park and ride rides. Then, the amount per ride is multiplied by the number of rides x, and the admission fee is added. Therefore, the equation for Play World is $y = 1.15x + 25.95$ and Fun Land is $y = 1.25x + 19.95$. To solve the system $y = 1.15x + 25.95$ and $y = 1.25x + 19.95$, the first equation can be substituted into the second equation for y and solved for x; $1.15x + 25.95 = 1.25x + 19.95$; $6 = 0.1x$, $x = 60$. Now, $x = 60$ can be substituted into either equation and solve for y; $y = 1.15(60) + 25.95$, $y = 94.95$. The solution to the system is (60 rides, $94.95).

The Elimination Method, p. 109

13. B A system of equations has infinite solutions when each equation has the same slope and the same y-intercept. Solve each equation for y: $4x - 4y = 12$ becomes $y = x - 3$ which has a slope 1 and y-intercept -3; $7x - 7y = 21$ becomes $y = x - 3$ which has a slope 1 and y-intercept -3.

14. G Since $(-8, -8)$ is the solution of the system, substitute this point into the second equation and solve for c; $c(-8) + 5(-8) = -64$, so $c = 3$.

15.

To write the system of equations, the number of the student tickets x is multiplied by 5 and the number of adult tickets y is multiplied by 8. This expression is then set equal to $3,700 in tickets sales. The second equation is the sum of the number of student tickets sold (x) and the number of adult tickets sold (y) set equal to 500. Therefore, the equations are $5x + 8y = 3,700$ and $x + y = 500$. Multiply the second equation by -5 and add the two equations together to eliminate x.

$$
\begin{aligned}
5x + 8y &= 3,700 \\
-5x - 5y &= -2,500 \\
\hline
3y &= 1,200 \\
y &= 400
\end{aligned}
$$

The solution to the system is 400 adult tickets.

16. H Let x = the cost of a pair of jeans and y = the cost of a long-sleeve t-shirt. For each equation, the number of jeans bought times the cost plus the number of long sleeve t-shirts bought times the cost is on the left side of the equation. The right side of the equation is the total cost. Therefore, the equation for Robert is $5x + 9y = 376$ and the equation for Juan is $2x + 6y = 208$.

17. B To write the system of equations, the general formula of rate times time equals distance is used. Both equations would equal 1,200 miles (distance). The first equation's time is 5 hours while the second is 6 hours. For the first equation, the speed of the plane x is being helped by the speed of the wind y. For the second equation, the speed of the plane x is being hurt by the speed of the wind y. The equation for the trip with the wind is $5(x + y) = 1,200$ and the trip against the wind is $6(x - y) = 1,200$. To solve the system $5(x + y) = 1,200$ and $6(x - y) = 1,200$, the first equation can be divided by 5 to become $x + y = 240$ and the second equation can be divided by 6 to become $x - y = 200$. Add the two equations and the result is $2x = 440$ or $x = 220$. This result can be substituted into one of the equations and solve for y; $5(220 + y) = 1,200$, $5y = 100$, $y = 20$. The solution to the system is (220 mph, 20 mph). Flying 70 miles per hour faster with wind 10 miles per hour slower gives a flight time of $z[(220 + 70) + (20 - 10)] = 1,200$, or $z = 4$ hours.

Lesson 6.1

Functions, p. 111

1. D In order for the graph to represent a function, there must be exactly one output for each input.

2.

Substitute 250 for x in the function $f(x) = 0.49x + 44.95$. Simplify and round to the nearest dollar.

Grid answer: 167

3. B The cost to print 100 fliers can be found by substituting 100 for x in the function: $f(100) = 0.49(100) + 44.95 = \$93.95$.

4. J For every domain value, there must be one and only one range value.

5. D The only choice that does not represent a function is II because the inputs 4 and 1 each have more than one output. For every other choice, each input has exactly one output.

Linear and Quadratic Functions, p. 113

6. F To find $f(-2)$, replace x with -2 in the function $f(x) = x^2 - 5x + 6$ and simplify; $(-2)^2 - 5(-2) + 6 = 4 + 10 + 6 = 20$. Similarly, to find $g(-2)$, replace x with -2 in the function $g(x) = -\frac{1}{2}x + 3$ and simplify; $-\frac{1}{2}(-2) + 3 = 1 + 3 = 4$.

7. C If $h(-1) = 5$, then the input is -1 and the output is 5. This corresponds to the point $(-1, 5)$. Therefore the point $(5, -1)$ lies on the graph of $y = h^{-1}(x)$.

8. F Find $f(0), f(1), f(-1)$, and $f(2)$ by replacing x with 0, 1, -1, and -2 in the function $f(x) = 3x^2 - 4x + 1$ and simplifying each one. Then compare the outputs to determine which statement is true.

9. C Evaluate the function $f(\text{x}) = 3.18x$ for $x = 5$ and $x = 12$.

10. F The graph of $f(x) = 3.18x$ is a line. So, for every input there is exactly one output and for every output there is exactly one input, and this means the function is one-to-one.

11.

Substitute $t = 1.5$ into the function $h(t) = -4.9t^2 + 19.6t + 98$ and simplify; $-4.9(1.5)^2 + 19.6(1.5) + 98 = 116.375$. Then substitute $t = 2.5$ into the function and simplify; $-4.9(2.5)^2 + 19.6(2.5) + 98 = 116.375$. Find the difference between the two heights; $116.375 - 116.375 = 0$.

Grid answer: 0

Functions in the Coordinate Plane, p. 115

12.

Because $x = -3$ lies in the domain of the piece $f(x) = -5x - 3$, evaluate this function when $x = -3$; $f(-3) = -5(-3) - 3 = 15 - 3 = 12$.

A grid-in answer of 12 is bubbled.

13. **A** Evaluate the function when $x = -2$, 0, and 2. For this function, $f(-2) = 10$, $f(0) = -4$, and $f(2) = -2$. The table that matches these values is A.

14. **J** Evaluating $f(x)$ at the x-values -1, 0, and 1 gives the points $(-1, -5)$, $(0, -3)$, and $(1, -1)$ on the graph of $f(x)$. Therefore, $(-5, -1)$, $(-3, 0)$, and $(-1, 1)$ are on the graph of $f^{-1}(x)$.

15. **B** On the first day of his training, Marcus runs an additional 10%, or $8 \times 0.1 = 0.8$ miles, for a total of $8.8 = 8 \times (1.1)1$ miles. The second day, he runs an additional 10%, or $8.8 \times 0.1 = 0.88$ miles, a total of 9.68, which equals $8 \times (1.1)^2$ miles. On the third day, Marcus runs an additional 10%, or 0.968, miles, for a total of 10.648 miles, which equals $8 \times (1.1)^3$ miles. On the dth day, he runs a total of $8 \times (1.1)^d$ miles.

16. **G** Evaluating the function at $x = 1$ shows that $(1, 9)$ is on the graph. B is the only graph that contains the point $(1, 9)$.

Lesson 6.2

Evaluating Linear and Quadratic Functions, p. 117

1. **B** Make a table of values for consecutive integer values of x. Then find the consecutive differences for the y values by subtracting. The first consecutive differences are common; 3.

2. **H** Make a table of values for consecutive integer values of x. Then find the consecutive differences. The second consecutive differences are common; 4.

3. **D** The membership charge is $1,000, which is the cost to play 0 rounds of golf. Playing 1 round of golf costs $15, for a total of $1,015.

4. **H** The cost to play r rounds of golf is $15r$. Adding in the membership fee makes the total cost C equal to $15r + 1,000$.

5. **B** Evaluate $f(0) = -8$. This eliminates graphs C and D. Evaluate $f(1) = 12 + 2(1) - 8 = -5$. This eliminates graph A. So graph B is correct.

6.   For consecutive integer values of x, $y = 11$. Therefore the first consecutive differences are common; 0.

Grid answer: 0

7.   B   The second consecutive differences of a linear function are equal to 0, so A is linear. C and D show common second consecutive differences, so they are quadratic.

8.   G   Make a table of values for consecutive integer values of x. Then find the consecutive differences. The second consecutive differences are common; -12.

9.   C   In $p(t)$, substitute 32 for h, 16 for v, and 32 for a. Simplify to write the function $p(t) = -16t^2 + 16t + 32$. Note that $p(1) = 32$; C is the only table that shows this.

10.   J   The first two consecutive differences were calculated incorrectly and are also equal to -1. Bobby subtracted consecutive y-values in the wrong order when calculating these two values.

Recognizing Linear and Quadratic Functions, p. 121

11.   A   The first consecutive differences are common and are equal to 4.

12.   H   None of the first, second, or third consecutive differences are common, so the function is not linear, quadratic, or of degree 3.

13.   B   The second consecutive differences are common and are equal to 2.

14.   H   The table for the *Volley* does not show a common consecutive difference.

15.   Make a table of values for consecutive integer values of x. Then find the consecutive differences. The fourth consecutive differences are common; 24.

Grid answer: 2 4

16.   G   Since the fourth consecutive differences are common, the degree is 4.

17. If the nth consecutive differences are common, then n is the degree.

(Grid-in answer: 3)

18. G Brenda is correct that simple interest is a linear relationship. However, although the graph appears to be a line, finding the first consecutive differences shows that the function is not linear.

19. D If the third consecutive differences are all equal to 0, then the second consecutive differences are common, and therefore the function is quadratic.

20. J Use the graph to make a table of values for consecutive integer values of x. Find the consecutive differences. The first consecutive differences are common and are equal to 3.

Lesson 6.3

Key Features, p. 125

1. B A linear function is a graph in the form of the line. The x-intercept is the value where the graph crosses the x-axis, and the y-intercept is the value where the graph crosses the y-axis. The other options are either not lines, or do not cross the x-axis at -4.

2. From the graph, the vertex is at the point of $(1, 16)$. The axis of symmetry contains the x-coordinate of the vertex and is a vertical line. The equation of the line is $x = 1$.

(Grid-in answer: 1)

3. B The x-intercept of a graph is the value where the graph crosses the x-axis. The graph crosses the x-axis at -3 and 5.

4. J If $y = (ax + b)(cx + d)$ is the factored form of a quadratic, then the product bd is the constant of the quadratic and the constant is the y-intercept of the graph. This graph crosses the y-axis at 15 and therefore the constant coefficient of the function is $bd = 15$.

5. C The values of increasing and decreasing are described by the x values of the graph. In the graph, the function is decreasing for all values of x less than -1 and all values greater than 5 because the graph is falling from left to right in those intervals. The graph is increasing or rising from left to right for the x values between -1 and 5.

6. G The function in expanded form is $y = ax^2 + (b - ac)x - bc$. The coefficient of x^2 in the function is a, which is positive. A quadratic function with a positive leading coefficient increases indefinitely on both the left and right ends.

7. The relative maxima are at $x = -5$, 0, and 6 and the y-values that correspond to those x's are 6, 2, and 2. The sum is $6 + 2 + 2 = 10$.

Grid-in answer: 1 0

8. The smallest relative minimum is determined by the lowest value in a particular section of a graph. The largest relative maximum is determined by the highest value in a particular section of a graph. The graph's lowest point has a y-value of -10. The graph's highest point has a y-value of 6. The difference is $6 - (-10) = 16$.

Grid-in answer: 1 6

9. B The graph has symmetry that is rotational since the graph will coincide with itself after a rotation of $180°$ around $(0, 5)$.

10. H Substitute the vertex $(2, -4)$ into the vertex form, $y = a(x - 2)^2 - 4$, and simplify: $y = a(x^2 - 4x + 4) - 4$. If $a = 3$, then $y = 3(x^2 - 4x + 4) - 4$ which simplifies to $y = 3x^2 - 12x + 8$. None of the other values for a simplify to one of the given equations.

11. A The line of symmetry for a parabola is at the midpoint between the two zeros of the graph. The quadratic equation $y = -2x^2 + 12x - 10$ factors as $y = -2(x - 1)(x - 5)$ and therefore has zeros at $x = 1$ and $x = 5$. The midpoint of the zeros is $x = 3$.

Use Key Features to Draw a Graph, p. 130

12. J The other choices cross either the y-axis or the x-axis at the wrong place on the graph.

13. A The other choices have either a negative x-intercept or negative y-intercept or both.

14. J The other choices either extend up indefinitely in both directions or have an incorrect x-intercept.

15. C The other choices either extend down indefinitely or have an incorrect x- or y-intercept.

16. H The other choices either have incorrect intervals of increase and decrease or the incorrect relative maximum.

17. B A negative y-intercept means that b must be negative. With a positive x-intercept, the slope will be positive, or m will be positive.

18. F The function is a quadratic, which has the same end behavior on both ends. Since the coefficient of the x^2 term is positive, the graph extend up to the left and up to the right indefinitely.

Lesson 6.4

Compare Proportional Relationships, p. 133

1. B The unit rate for biking is 8 calories per minute. So biking for 4 minutes would result in burning $8 \times 4 = 32$ calories not 30 calories.

2.

E-Your Book pays \$1 for every 20 books downloaded, or $\frac{100}{20} = \$0.05$ per book. Kimberly must sell $\frac{20}{0.05} = 400$ books.

3. D Sell Your Book company will pay Kimberly 20 cents for every book sold, so $100 \times 0.20 = \$20$. E-Your Book company will pay Kimberly \$1 for every 20 books downloaded, so $100 \div 20 = 5$ and $5 \times \$1 = \$5$. \$5 does not equal \$20.

4. E F, G and H are true. In H, her statement is accurate that $\frac{1}{10}$ of a loop in a minute is faster than $\frac{1}{20}$ of a loop in a minute. This is not a correct result for this problem but the statement itself is accurate. In F using a ratio is fine for this problem. So saying that Ann should not have used a ratio is incorrect. She just happened to use the incorrect ratios.

Compare Linear Functions, p. 136

5. C The costs for 10 pounds of almonds for Fresh Day grocery is $3(10) + 2 = \$32$. For Friendly Earth, it is $2(10) + 3 = \$23$. The average is $\frac{32 + 23}{2} = \$27.50$. Thus, the price per pound should be $\frac{27.5}{10} = \$2.75$.

6. G The number of pounds of almonds purchased (p) would be the amount spent (s) minus the container fee (2), divided by the price per pound (\$3), or $p = \frac{s - 2}{3}$.

7.

The table shows a linear function with a common difference of 2. So, \$2 is the unit rate.

8.

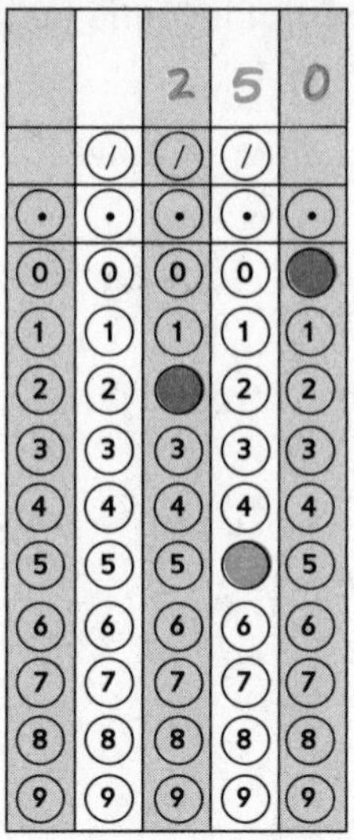

The answer is **250** (filled-in grid shows 2, 5, 0).

$130 - 190 = -60$. So $190 + 60 = 250$.

9. A Lisa still had 20 miles left to cross the state line when she had been driving for 4 hours, $f(4) = -70(4) + 300 = -280 + 300 = 20$ miles.

10. H Barbara will be paid $\dfrac{3{,}200 - 2{,}400}{120 - 80} = \dfrac{800}{40}$. So Barbara gets paid $800 per 40 hours or per week, not $1600 a week.

11. D Item One costs $3,500 and Item Two costs $3,600 when 100 items are made. So Item Two costs more.

Compare Quadratic Functions, p. 139

12. J Looking at the graph, the maximum for the quadratic function is 64. So Mrs. Bott's golf ball reaches a maximum height of 64 feet.

13. A Mrs. Bott's golf ball only stays in the air for 3 seconds (read the graph where $y = 0$) while Mr. Bott's stays in the air for 8 seconds (using the quadratic formula).

14 H Using the quadratic formula with $a = -16$, $b = 120$, and $c = 64$, the x-intercepts are -0.5 and 8. Since -0.5 corresponds to negative time, the value of 8 is when his ball hit the ground.

15. C Look at the table for the newer book. At 16 weeks, total weekly profit is 28. The profit is in thousands of dollars so the answer is $28,000.

16. G The older book starts making a profit after 2 weeks and the newer book starts making a profit after 9 weeks. So, the older book starts making a profit before the newer book.

Lesson 7.1

Rectangles, p. 141

1. D The area of the driveway is $(35 \times 24) = 840$ ft^2. The cost of one coat is 840 ft$^2 \times \dfrac{\$18.50}{420 \text{ ft}^2} = \$37.00$. Two coats will cost $2 \times \$37.00 = \$74.00$.

2.

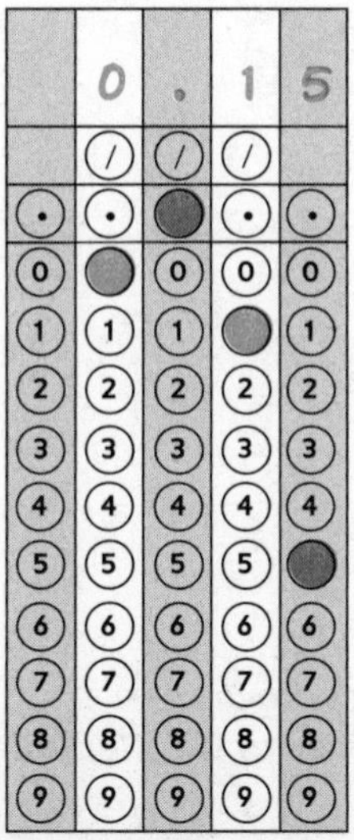

The answer is **0.15** (filled-in grid shows 0, ., 1, 5).

The area of a rectangle equals its length times its width; $0.3 \times 0.5 = 0.15$.

3. **B**   A reasonable unit of measurement for the length and height of a wall is feet. An area quantity is found by multiplying two length measurements. Therefore, the best unit of measurement is square feet.

4. **G**   The perimeter of the school is $2(80) + 2(52) = 264$ ft. Dividing $\frac{5,280}{264} = 20$, which is the number of times a student must run around the school in order to have run a mile.

5. **D**   The dimensions involved are the height, 10 in., and the front to back measurement, 12 in. The total length of the ribbon needed is $2(10) + 2(12) = 44$ in.

6. **G**   The formula for the area of a rectangle is $A = \ell w$. Substitute the given information into the formula and solve for ℓ; $1,140 = \ell(30)$ so $\ell = 38$ cm.

7. **B**   The formula for the perimeter of a rectangle is $P = 2\ell + 2w$. The formula for the area is $A = \ell w$. Since they are equal, $2\ell + 2w = \ell w$. Substituting $\ell = 6$, we have $2(6) + 2w = (6)w$ and now solve for w.

8.

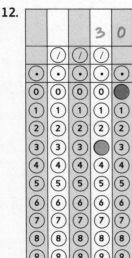

The length and width must be factor pairs of 24. The possible pairs are 1×24, 2×12, 3×8, and 4×6. The largest perimeter would be $2(1) + 2(24) = 50$ cm.

9. **C**   The total distance of 17 mi north, 23 mi east, 17 mi south, and 23 mi west is 80 mi.

Triangles, p. 143

10. **H**   The area of a triangle is $A = \frac{1}{2}bh$. Substitute into the formula the known information, $7.5 = \frac{1}{2}(3)h$ and solve for $h = 5$ m.

11. **C**   Use the Pythagorean Theorem $c^2 = 8^2 + 15^2$ to find the length of the missing side, c. Then find the sum $8 + 15 + 17$ to get the perimeter, 40 yd.

12.

Use the Pythagorean Theorem $13^2 = 5^2 + b^2$ to find the length of the missing base, b. After solving for b, find the area; $A = \frac{1}{2}(12)(5) = 30$ mm².

13. **C**   If the triangle is isosceles, the lengths must be either 8-8-3 or 8-3-3. But 8-3-3 will not work, because the 3-in. sides will not meet in the middle to form a third vertex if they are each attached to the ends of the 8-in. side. So, $8 + 8 + 3 = 19$ in.

14. F Use the Pythagorean Theorem to solve for b; $15^2 + b^2 = 25^2$; $b^2 = 25^2 - 15^2$; $b^2 = 625 - 225$; $b^2 = 400$; $b = 20$ ft.

15.

The perimeter of a triangle is equal to the sum of all three sides. So, $27 = a + 7 + 9$. Solve for $a = 11$ units.

16. J The three legs of the trip form a right triangle. By the Pythagorean Theorem, $180^2 + 240^2 = c^2$, where c is the length of the third leg of the trip, 300 miles. The time for the trip is the perimeter of the triangle (total distance) in miles divided by the speed in miles per hour; $t = \dfrac{180 + 240 + 300}{120} = 6$ hr after the departing time of noon.

17. B The two shorter sides of the right triangle are the base and the height. According to the formula for the area of a triangle, $24 = \frac{1}{2}bh$, so $b(8) = 48$ and $b = 6$. If the two legs measure 6 in. and 8 in., then the longest leg is 10 in. using the Pythagorean Theorem.

Parallelograms and Trapezoids, p. 146

18. G To find the height, use the Pythagorean Theorem; $h^2 + 7^2 = 25^2$. Solve for $h = 24$ ft. Now, substitute the information into the area formula for a parallelogram; $A = bh = (7)(24) = 168$ ft^2.

19. D Substitute the information into the area formula for a trapezoid $\left(A = \frac{1}{2}h(b_1 + b_2)\right)$; $35 = \frac{1}{2}(5)(3 + b_2)$. Solve for b_2, the length of the other base; $70 = (5)(3 + b_2)$; $14 = (3 + b_2)$; $11 = b_2$.

20. H The perimeter is the sum of the side lengths; $9 + 7 + 9 + 7 = 32$ m. The height is irrelevant.

21. B The area in Position A is 9×15 in^2. In Position B, by the Pythagorean Theorem, $h^2 + 9^2 = 15^2$, so $h = 12$ and therefore the area is 9×12 in^2. So, the difference in their areas is $135 - 108 = 27$ in^2.

22. F The area of the parallelogram is $4 \text{ mm} \times 6 \text{ mm} = 24$ mm^2. So $8 \text{ mm} \times h = 24$ mm^2 also. Now solve for $h = 3$ mm.

23.

Since the area is given, the height is a variable to solve in the formula for area. So, $\left(A = \frac{1}{2}h(b_1 + b_2)\right)$ and $104 = \frac{1}{2}h(7 + 19)$ gives that $h = 8$ cm.

Answer Key

24. H $18 - 12 = 6$, $6^2 + 8^2 = 100$, $\sqrt{100} = 10$, so opposite side is 10 in.

25. B Area of the trapezoid $= \frac{1}{2}(18 + 12)(8) = 120$ in.^{2}

Lesson 7.2

Circumference, p. 149

1. B The circumference of the racetrack is $2 \times \left(\frac{600}{2}\right) \times 3.14 = 1{,}884$ ft.

2. G The distance by going around the border of the park is half the circumference of the circle; $\frac{1}{2}(800)(3.14)$ m. Therefore, the difference in distance between going around and through the park is $\frac{1}{2}(800)(3.14) - 800 \approx 456$ m.

3. B The distance traveled in 1 revolution, or the circumference of the wheel, is $3.14d$, where d is the diameter. In 475 revolutions, the distance traveled will be $475 \times 3.14d$, so $1{,}000 = 475 \times 3.14d$. Solving for d, $d = 0.67$ and the diameter is 0.67, or 0.7 meters.

4.

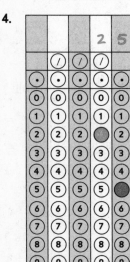

The circumference of the large gear is $(2)(3.14)5$ inches, and the circumference of the small gear is $(2)(3.14)3$ inches. In 15 rotations, a point on the large gear moves $15(10)(3.14)$ inches. Divide $15(10)(3.14)$ by the circumference of the small gear $(6)(3.14)$ inches to find the number of times the small gear will turn; $\frac{15(10)(3.14)}{6(3.14)} = 25$ times.

5. D After 15 seconds, the ripple will have grown to a radius of $2(15) = 30$ ft. The circumference of the ripple is therefore $(2)(3.14)30 \approx 188$ ft.

Area, p. 151

6. G A circle with a diameter of 22 in. has a radius of 11 in. The area of the circle is therefore $A = \pi(11)^2 = 121\pi$ in.^{2}

7.

The area of the chef's current table is $(3.14)\left(\frac{15}{2}\right)^2$ in.^{2}. The table she needs has twice the area, or $2(3.14)\left(\frac{15}{2}\right)^2$ in.^{2}. Now, using the area formula with this new area, solve for the radius:

$2(3.14)\left(\frac{15}{2}\right)^2 = (3.14)r^2$; $2\left(\frac{15}{2}\right)^2 = r^2$; $r \approx 10.6$ in. The diameter is twice the radius, or $2(10.6) = 21.2$ in.

8.

The area of the top of the box is $(3.14)10^2$ in². Divide to find the number of packets needed; $[(3.14)(10^2)] \div 12 \approx 26.2$. So, 26 packets is not enough, and Gregor will need 27 packets of glitter.

9. **A**   The area of the smaller circle is $(3.14)(7^2) \approx 154$ m².

10. **H**   A circle with a circumference of 18π cm has a diameter of 18 cm and a radius of 9 cm. Therefore, the area of this circle is $\pi(9)^2 = 81\pi$ cm².

11. **C**   The diameter is given, but the formula for area is in terms of the radius. Stefan's pizza has a radius of 5 in., and therefore the area is $\pi(5)^2 = 25\pi$ in², not 100π in².

Find Radius or Diameter, p. 153

12. **H**   The height of the seat halfway through a revolution is equal to the diameter of the Ferris wheel plus the height of the lowest seat. Use the circumference formula to solve for d: $126 = 3.14d$; $d \approx 40$ ft. Now add the 10 feet off the ground and the total is 50 ft.

13. **A**   Four laps around the track is 4 times the circumference, so the circumference is $5{,}280 \div 4 = 1{,}320$ ft. Use the circumference formula to solve for d: $1{,}320 = 3.14d$; $d \approx 420$ ft. So, the radius of the track is $420 \div 2 = 210$ ft.

14. **H**   Two pounds of grass seed can cover $2 \times 400 = 800$ ft². Use the area formula to solve for r: $800 = 3.14r^2$; $r \approx 16$ ft.

15. **B**   A pizza with an 8-inch diameter has an area of $\pi4^2$ in². Since 2 cups of flour makes enough dough for $\pi4^2$ in², 1 cup of flour will make enough dough for $\frac{\pi4^2}{2}$ in², and 4.5 cups will make enough dough for $4.5\left(\frac{\pi4^2}{2}\right)$ in². Use the area formula to solve for r; $\pi r^2 \, 4.5\left(\frac{\pi4^2}{2}\right) = 36\pi$; $r = 6$ in., so $d = 12$ in.

16. **G**   The figure is formed by a square with side lengths s and two semicircles with radius $\frac{1}{2}s$. The area of the square is s^2 cm² and the area of the two semicircles is $3.14\left(\frac{1}{2}s\right)^2$ cm². Set the sum of these two areas equal to the given area, and solve for s: $28.6 = s^2 + 3.14\left(\frac{1}{2}s\right)^2$; $28.6 = s^2\left(1 + \frac{1}{4}(3.14)\right)$; $16.02 \approx s^2$; $s \approx 4$ cm.

Lesson 7.3

Rectangular Prisms, p. 155

1. **B**   The volume of the rectangular prism divided by its height gives the product of its width and length, which is the area of the base. The area of the base is then $\frac{x^3 + 6x^2 + 9x}{x} = x^2 + 6x + 9$. Since $x^2 + 6x + 9 = (x + 3)^2$, the side length of the square base is $(x + 3)$. Therefore the surface area of the prism is $4x(x + 3) + 2(x + 3)^2$.

Answer Key

2.

The grid shows the answer **18**.

If l is the length of the container and the length is 3 times the width, then $l = 3w$. Also, $16 = l + w = 3w + w = 4w$. So, $w = 4$ mm. Therefore, the width is 4 mm and the length is 12 mm. Substitute $V = 864$, $w = 4$, and $l = 12$ in the formula $V = l \cdot w \cdot h$. Then solve for h.

3. **B** To determine the amount of cement necessary, find the volume of the prism. First, all measurements must be converted to the same units. The depth is 18 inches = 1.5 feet. The volume of the prism is $V = length \cdot width \cdot height = 50 \times 16 \times 1.5 = 1,200 \text{ ft}^3$. The number of bags of cement needed is then $\frac{1,200}{0.6} = 2,000$ and the number of pounds of concrete is $2,000 \times 80 = 160,000$.

4. **H** Multiply the length, width, and height of the box.

5.

The grid shows the answer **665.5**.

To find the surface area of the box, find the sum of the areas of all six sides of the box.

Cylinders and Prisms, p. 157

6. **G** To find how much the can is able to hold, you must find the volume of the cylinder. The formula for the volume of a cylinder is $V = \pi r^2 h$.

7.

You must determine the surface area of the cylinder minus the area of the bases. The area of this region is $\pi \cdot diameter \cdot height$. Substitute 3.14 for π, 8 for diameter, and 20 for height and evaluate.

8. J To find the volume of a prism, find the area of the base (in this case the right triangle) and multiply it by the height of the prism.

9. A The volume of the prism is $\frac{1}{2}(b \times 8)(b \times 15)(3 \times 20) = 14{,}400$. Solving for b gives $b^2 = 4$, so $b = 2$.

10. H To find the volume of the tent, calculate the area of the triangular base and multiply it by the height of the tent; $\frac{1}{2} \cdot 3 \cdot 2 \cdot 4 = 12$.

11. B You must find the surface area of the tent. Begin by finding the area of the three rectangular faces, and then find the area of the two triangular bases. Now, add all of the areas together. $2.5 \cdot 4 \cdot 2 + 3 \cdot 4 + 2 \cdot \frac{1}{2} \cdot 2 \cdot 3 = 38$.

Pyramids, Cones, and Spheres, p. 159

12. J The formula for the volume of a pyramid is $Volume = \frac{1}{3}(Area\ of\ base)(height)$. For this pyramid the base is a square. $V = \frac{1}{3} \cdot (12 \cdot 12) \cdot 8 = 384$.

13. B To calculate the surface area of the pyramid, you must find the area of each side of the pyramid. The pyramid is made up of four congruent triangles and one square base. In order to find the slant height of the pyramid, you must use the Pythagorean Theorem; $l^2 = 6^2 + 8^2$, $l = 10$. Now use the surface area formula for a pyramid, $SA = \frac{1}{2}Pl + B$. Making all the substitutions, $SA = \frac{1}{2} \cdot (4 \cdot 12) \cdot 10 + 12 \cdot 12 = 384$.

14. F The formula for the volume of a cone is $Volume = \frac{1}{3}\pi(radius)^2(height)$. Substitute $r = 5$, $h = 12$, and 3.14 for π. Then simplify.

15. C The formula for the surface area of a cone is $Volume = \pi(radius)(slant\ height) + \pi(radius)^2$. First you must find the slant height by using the Pythagorean Theorem. Then substitute $r = 5$ for radius, $l = 13$, and 3.14 for π and simplify.

16. H The formula for the volume of a sphere is $Volume = \frac{4}{3}\pi(radius)^3$. Substitute 3.14 for π and $r = 5$ and simplify. The volume is $523.\frac{1}{3}$ cubic inches. The density given must be converted to pounds per square inch: $\frac{0.58}{16} \approx 0.03625$. Therefore the number of pounds of water is $523.33 \times 0.03625 = 18.97$.

17. A Cutting off one of the corners would result in cutting through 3 of the edges of the prism, which would create a triangle.

18. H Any plane that intersects the prism parallel to the base intersects at a rectangle the same shape as the base. Therefore, the area is $10 \times 3 = 30$ cm^2.

Lesson 7.4

2-Dimensional Figures, p. 161

1. A The perimeter is the distance around the outside of the figure. For this composite figure, it is the sum of two sides of the triangle, two sides of the square, and the distance around the semicircle:

$$10 + 10 + 7 + 7 + \left(\frac{1}{2}\right)(3.14)(7) \approx 34 + 10.99 \approx 44.99.$$

Answer Key

2. **F** Find the sum of the areas of the triangle, square, and semicircle.

$$A_{triangle} = \left(\frac{1}{2}\right)(9.4)(7) = 32.9$$

$$A_{square} = (7)(7) = 49$$

$$A_{semicircle} \approx \left(\frac{1}{2}\right)(3.14)(3.5)^2 \approx 19.2325$$

Total Area $\approx 32.9 + 49 + 19.2325 \approx 101.13$

3. **D** To find the perimeter of the figure, add up the lengths of all the sides of the figure. There are 2 sides with a length of 12 and 14 sides with a length of 3: $2(12) + 14(3) = 66$.

4.

The figure can be broken up into 1 large rectangle with dimensions 9 inches by 12 inches, and 4 small squares with sides of length 3 inches. To find the area of the figure, find the sum of the areas of all of its parts: $(9)(12) + 4(3)(3) = 108 + 36 = 144$.

Answer gridded: 1 4 4

5.

First find the perimeter of the garden. Use Pythagorean Theorem to find the equal side lengths of the triangle. *Perimeter* $\approx 8 + 6 + 5 + 5 + \left(\frac{1}{2}\right)(3.14)(6) \approx 33.42$ The perimeter of the garden is approximately 33.42 feet. To determine the cost of the lining, multiply this by the cost per foot, \$6; $33.42 \cdot 6 \approx 200.52$. The nearest dollar is \$201.

Answer gridded: 2 0 1

6. **H** Find the area of the garden.

$$A_{triangle} = \frac{1}{2}(3)(8) = 12$$

$$A_{rectangle} = (6)(8) = 48$$

$$A_{semicircle} \approx \left(\frac{1}{2}\right)(3.14)(3)^2 \approx 14.13$$

Total Area $\approx 12 + 48 + 14.13 \approx 74.13$ square feet

To determine the approximate cost for the soil and mulch, multiply the total area by \$10. $74.13 \cdot 10 = 741.30$

Volume of 3-Dimensional Solids, p. 164

7. **C**   Find the sum of the volumes of the square pyramid and the prism.

$$V_{pyramid} = \left(\frac{1}{3}\right)(8)^2(3) = 64$$

$$V_{prism} = (8)(8)(5) = 320$$

$$Total\ Volume = 64 + 320 = 384$$

8. **G**   Find the sum of the volumes of the square pyramid and the cube. The side of the cube is $8\left(2\frac{1}{2}\right) = 20$ cm.

$$V_{pyramid} = \left(\frac{1}{3}\right)(20)^2(8) = 1{,}066.\overline{6}$$

$$V_{cube} = (20)^3 = 8{,}000$$

$$Total\ Volume = 1{,}066.\overline{6} + 8{,}000 = 9066.\overline{6}$$

9. **D**   Find the volume of the cylinder and the two hemispheres and add them together. The two hemispheres have the same radius, so you can find the volume of a sphere with a radius of 2 mm.

$$V_{cylinder} \approx (3.14)(2)^2(10) \approx 125.6$$

$$V_{sphere} \approx \left(\frac{4}{3}\right)(3.14)(2)^3 \approx 33.49$$

$$Total\ Volume \approx 125.6 + 33.94 \approx 159.09$$

10.

Find the sum of the volumes of the cylinder and the hemisphere. The height of the hemisphere (radius) is 15 feet.

$$V_{cylinder} \approx (3.14)(15)^2(45) \approx 31{,}792.5$$

$$V_{hemisphere} \approx \left(\frac{1}{2}\right)\left(\frac{4}{3}\right)(3.14)(15)^3 \approx 7{,}065$$

$$Total\ Volume \approx 31{,}792.5 + 7{,}065 \approx 38{,}857.5$$

11. **C**   Find the sum of the volumes of the cone and the cylinder. The height of the cone is 12 cm.

$$V_{cone} \approx \left(\frac{1}{3}\right)(3.14)(5)^2(12) \approx 314$$

$$V_{cylinder} \approx (3.14)(5)^2(24) \approx 1{,}884$$

$$Total\ Volume \approx 3.14 + 1{,}884 \approx 2{,}198$$

12. **G**   The formula for the volume of a cylinder is $V = \pi r^2 h$. If r is tripled the resulting volume will be $\pi(3r)^2 h = \pi(9r^2)h = 9\pi r^2 h$. Thus, the new cylinder will have a volume that is nine times the original cylinder.

Surface Area of 3-Dimensional Solids, p. 166

13. **C**   To find the surface area, you must add up the areas of all of the sides of the figure. In this figure, there are 1 square, 4 congruent rectangles, and 4 congruent triangles.

$$A_{square} = (8)(8) = 64$$

$$A_{rectangles} = 4(8)(5) = 160$$

$$A_{triangles} = 4\left(\frac{1}{2}\right)(8)(5) = 80$$

$$Total\ Area = 64 + 160 + 80 = 304.$$

14. H To determine how much paint is necessary, you must first calculate the surface area to be painted. The two bases of the cylinder will not be painted.

$$SA_{cylinder} \approx (3.14)(30)(45) \approx 4{,}239$$

$$SA_{hemisphere} \approx \left(\frac{1}{2}\right)(4)(3.14)(15)^2 \approx 1{,}413$$

Then divide the total surface area to be painted by 400 and round the answer up to the nearest whole number so that the farmer has enough paint.

$$4{,}239 + 1{,}413 = 5{,}652$$

$$\frac{5{,}652}{400} \approx 14.13$$

So, 15 gallons of paint are needed.

15. C Find the surface area of the two hemispheres, which is one sphere with a radius of 2 mm. The surface area of the cylinder does not include the two bases.

$$SA_{hemisphere} \approx 4(3.14)(2)^2 \approx 50.24$$

$$SA\_cylinder \approx (3.14)(4)(10) \approx 125.6$$

Total surface area $= 50.24 + 125.6 = 175.84$, rounding to the nearest whole number 176 mm^2.

16. H For the cone, the area of the base is not necessary, and the area of only one base of the cylinder is needed.

$$SA_{cone} \approx (3.14)(5)(13) \approx 204.1$$

$$SA_{cylinder} \approx (3.14)(10)(24) + (3.14)(5)^2 \approx 832.1$$

Total surface area $= 204.1 + 832.1 = 1{,}036.2$, rounding up to the nearest whole number 1,037 cm^2.

Each roll of wrapping paper contains 4 square meters $= 4 \times 100 \times 100 = 40{,}000$ square centimeters of paper.

Thus 100 boxes of perfume would require $\frac{(100 \times 1{,}037)}{40{,}000} \approx 2.6$. Rounding to a whole number of rolls is 3 rolls.

17. D The rotation produces a cylinder with a radius of 4 inches and a height of 5 inches. Therefore, the volume of the cylinder is $V = 5 \times \pi \times 4^2 = 80\pi$.

18. H A circle rotated about any line through its center by 180° produces a sphere.

19. D Each smaller square face has an area of $\left(\frac{3}{4}\right)^2 = \frac{9}{16}$. With 9 smaller squares per large face and 6 total faces, the total surface area is $9 \times 6 \times \frac{9}{16} = \frac{486}{16} = 30\frac{3}{8}$.

Lesson 8.1

Measures of Central Tendency, p. 169

1. B To calculate the mean, find the sum of the data set and then divide that sum by the number of data values. The sum is 573 and there are 15 numbers in the data set; $573 \div 15 = 38.2$.

2. F Adding 60 to the data set gives a new sum of 633 of the date set and adds another data value; $633 \div 16 \approx 39.6$ (rounded to the nearest tenth).

3. C The number 44 appears the most in both data sets, making it the mode for both data sets.

4.

The median of a data set is the middle number when all values are ordered from least to greatest.

5.

| | | | 1 | 3 |

The range is the difference between the largest value in the data set and the smallest value in the data set; $44 - 31 = 13$.

6. J In a data set with an even number of items, the median is the average of the two middle numbers when the set is ordered from least to greatest.

Finding a Missing Data Item, p. 171

7. D Since Amy wants to earn an average of 84% or better on four tests, her test scores need to add up to 336 $(84 \cdot 4 = 336)$. The sum of her already earned scores {78, 82, 86} is 246. And $336 - 246 = 90$, so she needs 90% on the fourth test.

8. H Since Dontell needs an average of $1,000 over an 8-week period, he needs his sales to total $8,000 $(1,000 \cdot 8 = 8,000)$. During weeks 1–7, his total sales were $7,028. Dontell needs to sell $8,000 - 7,028 = \$972$ in week 8 to receive the bonus.

9. B Since Allison wants her four test average to be 90%, the sum of her 4 test scores divided by 4 should equal at least 90.

10. J The sum of Wes's scores on six exams needs to be at least 510 $(85 \cdot 6 = 510)$. His test score sum on the first five tests is 414, therefore, Wes needs at least $510 - 414 = 96\%$ on the last test.

11.

| | | | 1 | 0 |

To average 7 hours per day, Karina needs to work a total of 35 hours in 5 days $(7 \cdot 5 = 35)$. She worked a total of 25 hours Monday–Thursday; therefore, she still needs to work $35 - 25 = 10$ hours on Friday.

Weighted Averages, p. 173

12. G The dot plot shows 18 x's, each of which represent a person surveyed. The data set for the number of jeans owned is: 0, 0, 1, 2, 2, 2, 3, 3, 3, 3, 4, 4, 4, 4, 4, 5, 5, 5. The mean is the average $(54 \div 18 = 3)$.

13. **A** Adding two more shoppers gives a total of 20 people surveyed. To average 2.75 jeans per person, the sum of the values in the data set needs to be 55 ($2.75 \cdot 20 = 55$). Since the sum was 54 before the two more shoppers were surveyed, only one new shopper must have a pair of jeans ($55 - 54 = 1$).

14. **G** To find the average price Tanya will charge for each session:
$75 \cdot 25 = \$1{,}875$; $\$150 \cdot 30 = \$4{,}500$; $\$200 \cdot 15 = \$3{,}000$
Total bookings: 70 ($25 + 30 + 15 = 70$)
Total charges: $9,375 ($\$1{,}875 + 4{,}500 + 3{,}000 = \$9{,}375$)
Average price: $\$9{,}375 \div 70 = \$133.93$

15. **A** To find the average price of an item sold:
$3 \cdot 30 = \$90$; $\$20 \cdot 12 = \$240$; $\$4 \cdot 40 = \$160$
Total items: 82 ($30 + 12 + 40 = 82$)
Total charges: $490 ($\$90 + \$240 + \$160 = \$490$)
Average price: $\$490 \div 82 = \$5.98$

16. **H** Miguel's final grade is calculated as:
$87 + 82 + 94 + 3(91) = 536$
$536 \div 6 = 89.3$

17. **C** The average profit per item is $(0.50)(7) + (0.30)(5) + (0.15)(4) + (0.05)(6) = 3.50 + 1.50 + 0.60 + 0.30 = 5.90$.

Lesson 8.2

Bar Graphs, p. 175

1. **C** Percent of increase is equal to $\dfrac{\text{new} - \text{original}}{\text{original}} \times 100\%$. The percent of increase in this case was $\dfrac{100{,}000 - 40{,}000}{40{,}000} \times 100\%$.

2.

The average sales will be $\dfrac{\$40{,}000 + \$100{,}000 + \$80{,}000 + \$q}{4}$, where q is the fourth-quarter sales in dollars. If the average sales reach $70,000, then $\dfrac{\$40{,}000 + \$100{,}000 + \$80{,}000 + \$q}{4} = \$70{,}000$. Solve for q to find the necessary fourth-quarter sales.

3. **B** Reading the bar graph, the interest on the 15-year mortgage would be about $115,000 while the interest on the 30-year mortgage would be about $270,000; $270{,}000 - 115{,}000 = \$155{,}000$.

4. **J** For a 30-year mortgage, look at the right-hand group of bars. Within those bars, look at the bar in the middle for a 9% mortgage.

5.

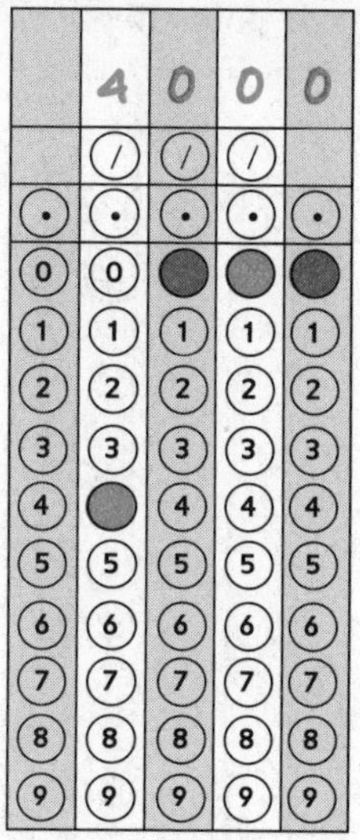

The total interest on a 30-year mortgage is a little less than $120,000. So the payment each year would be about $\frac{\$120,000}{30} = \$4,000$.

The answer grid shows: **4 0 0 0**

6. **G** Lines at every 5-dollar interval would be too thick and cluttered to read. Lines only at the 500-dollar or 1000-dollar mark would not give precise enough information. Lines at every 100-dollar interval are uncluttered and readable but also precise enough to be helpful.

7. **C** The graph is to give the number of riders in thousands, so the scale of the axis should include 0 to 85 to represent 50,000 to 85,000. The maximum value is 85, so the maximum value on the graph should be around 90. Answer C's graph extends to 200, which is unnecessary. The data will be concentrated towards the bottom of the graph, which could make the graph difficult to read.

Circle Graphs, p. 179

8.

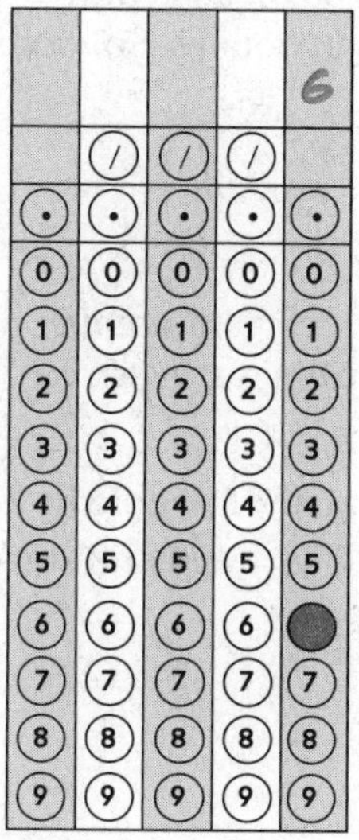

Gregg received 100% − 50% − 25% − 19% = 6% of the votes.

The answer grid shows: **6**

9. **C** A fifth is 20%; Pullam's support, at 19%, is close to that.

10. **J** Nothing in the chart reveals the total number of registered voters, so no percentage can be calculated.

11.

Answer: 1 2 5 5 0

Lee received 25%, or one-fourth, of the 50,200 votes cast, so the number of votes Lee received is $\frac{1}{4}(50{,}200) = 12{,}550$.

12. H Lee received half the votes of Wright. If Wright received the votes of $\frac{1}{3}$ of the registered voters, then the votes for Lee was $\frac{1}{2} \times \frac{1}{3} = \frac{1}{6}$ of the registered voters.

13. B "Car" is the largest segment in the circle graph; "Bus" is second.

14. J The ratio of housing to clothes is 28:9, which is close to 3:1.

15. D If their food cost takes up 22 cents out of every dollar, or 100 cents, then their cost for a month of food in which they earn \$3,875 will be $\frac{22}{100}(\$3{,}875)$ or $0.22(\$3{,}875) = \$852.50$.

16. F The difference between the housing and food budget is $0.28 - 0.22 = \$0.06$. Therefore, 0.06 on a certain amount of income should equal \$540; $0.06x = 540$, where x is the total monthly earnings in dollars. Solving, $x = \$9{,}000$.

17. A The total profit is listed as \$18,000. Therefore, the profit per quarter is $\frac{\$18{,}000}{4} = \$4{,}500$.

18. J The total profit is \$18,000 and 16.7% equals 0.167.

19. C The 3rd-quarter profits were about \$4,000; $0.222(\$18{,}000) = \$3{,}996$. If they increased by a certain number of dollars x, then the total profits also increased by x dollars, so the revised 3rd-quarter profits were 44% of the revised yearly total; $4{,}000 + x = 0.44(18{,}000 + x)$. Solve for x.

20. F The No and Undecided segments are all in reference to the Yes segment. Let x = the number of people in the Yes segment. Therefore, the equation $x + 2x + \frac{1}{3}x = 500$ represents the situation. Solving, $x = 150$ and since Undecided is $\frac{1}{3}x$, Undecided is 50 people.

Lesson 8.3

Dot Plots, p. 183

1. B The median is the middle number when the data values are written in order from least to greatest. In this dot plot with 11 points, this is represented by the dot that is 6 dots from the left (or 6 dots from the right). The median is 1.

2. H A survey of 55 people would have 5 times as many participants as the given survey. In the current survey, 2 out of 11 participants had 3 computers. The ratio could be expected to be the same in a larger survey, so $2 \times 5 = 10$.

3. There are 3 students with 2 computers at home, and 2 students with 3 computers at home. So, a total of 5 students have at least 2 computers at home.

4. H The dots in the dot plot translate to the data set 0, 0, 1, 1, 1, 1, 2, 2, 2, 3, 3.

5. B The additional data point would be represented in the dot plot by adding another dot above the data value 3, for a total of three dots. The tallest group of dots depicts the mode, which for this data set (with or without the additional data point) is the four dots above the data value 1.

Histograms, p. 185

6. G The intervals 15–19, 20–24, 25–29, and so on separate the data into 5-year intervals.

7. C Add the heights of the bars representing people 35 or older, which are the three rightmost bars: $4 + 2 + 1 = 7$ people.

8. J Add the heights of the bars representing people 29 or younger, which are the three leftmost bars: $3 + 9 + 15 = 27$ people. Out of a total of 40 people, $\frac{27}{40} = 0.675 = 67.5\%$ are under 30.

9. Subtract the sum of the bars for those in their thirties from the sum of the bars for those in their twenties: $(9 + 15) - (6 + 4) = 14$ mothers.

10. H In a group of 120 first-time mothers, the same percentages can be expected for each age range. In the given group of 40 first-time mothers, there are an equal number of first-time mothers in their teens and in their 40s. So it cannot be assumed that there would be more first-time mothers in their teens in the larger group.

Box Plots, p. 187

11. C In a box plot, the vertical bar within the box depicts the median. The median here is 14.

12. F The box plot gives the minimum value as 10 and the maximum value as 17. Therefore the range is $17 - 10 = 7$.

13.

Raul earns $12 per hour, or $12 × 10 = $120 in 10 hours. Caitlin earns $15 per hour, or $15 × 10 = $150 in 10 hours. So, Caitlin makes $150 − $120 = $30 more than Raul in 10 hours.

14. J The box plot shows minimum value 10, first quartile 12, median 14, third quartile 15, and maximum value 17. The only given data set that matches these values is choice D: 10, 11, 12, 13, 13, 14, 14, 15, 15, 16, 17.

15. B A dot plot visually divides a data set into fourths, with half of the data values falling between the first and third quartile. So, half of Henry's friends make between $12 and $15 per hour.

16. H Arrange the values in order from least to greatest to identify the five numbers needed to show the data set on a box plot: minimum (9), first quartile (11), median (25), third quartile (38), and maximum (45).

17. B Arrange the ten known data values in order from least to greatest: 4, 6, 8, 11, 12, 13, 14, 16, 18, 20. For a data set with eleven values, the 6th value is the median, and so the first quartile is the 3rd value and the third quartile is the 9th value. This data set has a first quartile of 8 and a third quartile of 16, so the unknown data value must fall between 8 and 16. Of the possible values shown, only $x = 10$ will force first and third quartiles to be as required.

Lesson 8.4

Tables, p. 189

1. D During week 3, there were 472 bacteria and 108 birds. To determine how many more bacteria than birds, subtract the two amounts: 472 − 108 = 364.

2. H Find the total of the ants and birds for the 4 weeks and compare it to the number of bacteria for each week. Week 1: 50 + 125 = 175; 175 > 8, Week 2: 147 + 119 = 266; 266 > 201, Week 3: 268 + 108 = 376; 376 < 472, Week 4: 319 + 102 = 421; 421 < 981. The number of bacteria was greater than the number of ants and birds combined in weeks 3 and 4.

3. B The variable x is located in the row for potatoes and the column for 2 sides. The cost for 2 sides of potatoes is $2.99.

4. J The variable y is located in the row for fruits and the column for 3 sides. The cost for 3 sides of fruits is $4.19.

5.

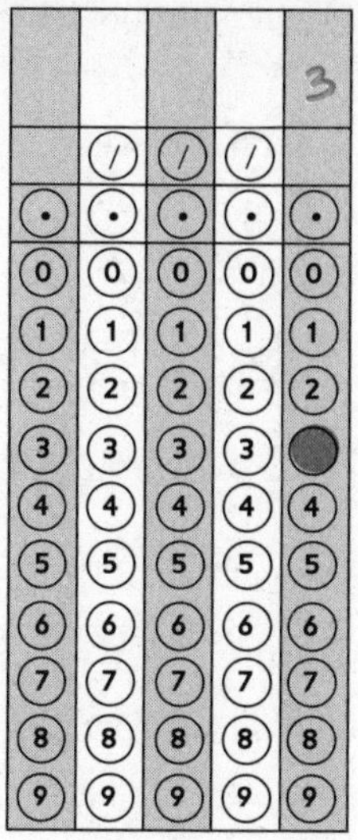

Answer gridded: 3

Since the columns represent the different designers, the rows will represent the different types of shirts. Since there are three different types of shirts, there should be 3 rows.

6. H   Find the sum for the rainfall for the months of April and May for each city.
Smithville: 8.3 + 4.7 = 13 inches; Jonesville: 5.7 + 6.3 = 12 inches;
Frankville: 6.6 + 4.2 = 10.8 inches; Robertville: 9.4 + 7.7 = 17.1 inches.
So Robertville had the most rainfall in April and May combined.

7. B   By looking at the data, Jonesville had two months in a row with less than 4 inches of rainfall (June and July). No other city did, so Jonesville is the answer.

8.

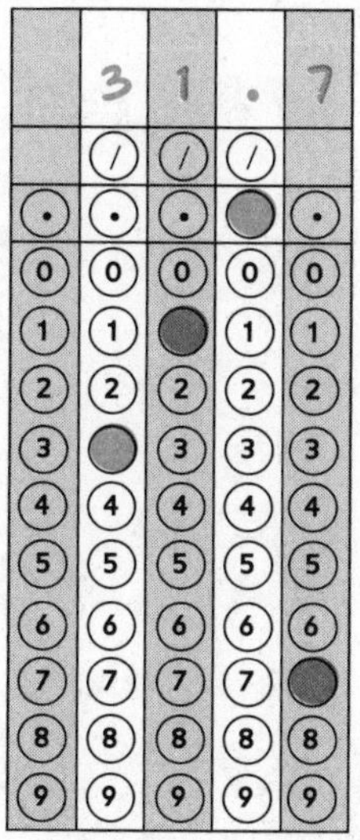

Answer gridded: 31.7

Find the sum of the rainfall for each month: 8.3 + 4.7 + 7.7 + 6.2 + 4.8 = 31.7.

Scatter Plots, p. 192

9. A   From the graph, the following points should be shown in the table: (72, 190), (74, 170), (75, 220), (76, 170), (77, 210), (78, 180), (80, 230), (82, 240), (83, 250), and (84, 200). This corresponds to the table in answer choice A.

10. G   Looking at the graph, there are 4 data points that have a y-value less than $450. Each data point represents one teenager; therefore 4 teenagers made less than $450. Out of the 10 teenagers represented in the graph, this is 40%.

11. C   One of the 18-year olds made $450. The other 18-year old made approximately $525. Therefore, together they made approximately 450 + 525 or $975.

Line Graphs, p. 194

12. H   Line graphs are good to use when showing how data might change over time. The number of inches of rainfall each month would make a good line graph.

13. A   The following points should be shown on the line graph (1998, 8), (2000, 6), (2002, 4), (2004, 12), (2006, 9), (2008, 5), (2010, 1), and (2012, 7). The graph in answer choice A shows all of these points.

14. H   Since there is no pattern to the data, no trend or conclusion can be made about the relationship between year and temperature.

15. B   The average temperature in 2004 was 12. The sum of the average temperatures in 2008 and 2012 is 12.

16. 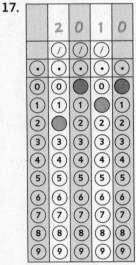   Using the table, the year 2004 had the highest average temperature of 12 degrees Celsius.

17.   The year 2010 had the lowest average temperature of 1 degree Celsius.

18. J   The amount of heating oil used and the number of mittens sold are likely to be positively correlated. When it is cold, more oil is used and sales of mittens would likely increase. However, an increase in the amount of heating oil used does not cause the number of mittens sold to increase or vice versa.

19. A   The temperature increases at a constant rate of 7 degrees for each additional hour of sunlight. Therefore the line of best fit is linear with a positive slope.

20. F   The line is decreasing approximately 2.5 for each 10 units in the x-axis, therefore a reasonable value for the slope is -0.25. The y-intercept is approximately $15 - (-0.25)(10) = 17.5$, so a reasonable line of best fit is $y = -0.25x + 18$.

Area of a	square	Area = side^2
	rectangle	Area = length × width
	triangle	Area = $\frac{1}{2}$ × base × height
	parallelogram	Area = base × height
	trapezoid	Area = $\frac{1}{2}$ × (base$_1$ + base$_2$) × height
	circle	Area = π × radius^2; π is approximately equal to 3.14
Perimeter of a	square	Perimeter = 4 × side
	rectangle	Perimeter = 2 × length + 2 × width
	triangle	Perimeter = side$_1$ + side$_2$ + side$_3$
Circumference of a	circle	Circumference = π × diameter; π is approximately equal to 3.14
Surface Area of a	rectangular/ right prism	Surface Area = 2(length × width) + 2(width × height) + 2(length × height)
	cube	6 × side^2
	square pyramid	Surface Area = ($\frac{1}{2}$ × perimeter of base × height of slant) + (base edge)^2
	cylinder	Surface Area = (2 × π × radius × height) + (2 × π × radius^2); π is approximately equal to 3.14
	cone	Surface Area = (π × radius × height of slant) + (π × radius^2)
	sphere	Surface Area = 4 × π × radius^2
Volume of a	rectangular/ right prism	Volume = length × width × height
	cube	Volume = edge^3
	square pyramid	Volume = $\frac{1}{3}$ × (base edge)^2 × height
	cylinder	Volume = π × radius^2 × height; π is approximately equal to 3.14
	cone	Volume = $\frac{1}{3}$ × π × radius^2 × height
	sphere	Volume = $\frac{4}{3}$ × π × radius^3

Coordinate Geometry	(x_1, y_1) and (x_2, y_2) are two points in a plane slope of a line $= \dfrac{y_2 - y_1}{x_2 - x_1}$; (x_1, y_1) and (x_2, y_2) are two points on the line slope-intercept form of the equation of a line $y = mx + b$, when m is the slope of the line and b is the y-intercept point-slope form of the equation of a line $y - y_1 = m\,(x - x_1)$, when m is the slope of the line
Pythagorean Theorem	$a^2 + b^2 = c^2$; in a right triangle, a and b are legs, and c is the hypotenuse
Quadratic Equations	standard form of a quadratic equation $ax^2 + bx + c = 0$ quadratic formula $x = \dfrac{-b \pm \sqrt{b^2 - 4ac}}{2a}$
Measures of Central Tendency	$\textbf{mean} = \dfrac{x_1 + x_2 + \ldots + x_n}{n}$, where the x's are the values for which a mean is desired, and n is the total number of values for x **median** = the middle value of an odd number of ordered values, and halfway between the two middle values of an even number of ordered values
Simple Interest	interest = principal $\times$ rate $\times$ time
Distance	distance = rate $\times$ time
Probability	**permutations:** $_nP_r = \dfrac{n!}{(n - r)!}$ **combinations:** $C(n, k) = \dfrac{P(n, k)}{k!}$ **independent events:** $P(A \text{ and } B) = P(A) \times P(B)$

Volume

Cylinder: $\qquad V = \pi r^2 h$

Pyramid: $\qquad V = \frac{1}{3}Bh$

Cone: $\qquad V = \frac{1}{3}\pi r^2 h$

Sphere: $\qquad V = \frac{4}{3}\pi r^3$

Coordinate Geometry

Midpoint formula: $\left(\dfrac{x_1 + x_2}{2}, \dfrac{y_1 + y_2}{2}\right)$

Distance formula:

$d = \sqrt{(x_2 - x_1)^2 + (y_2 - y_1)^2}$

Slope: $\quad m = \dfrac{y_2 - y_1}{x_2 - x_1}, x_2 \neq x_1$

Special Factoring

$a^2 - b^2 = (a - b)(a + b)$

$a^2 + 2ab + b^2 = (a + b)^2$

$a^2 - 2ab + b^2 = (a - b)^2$

$a^3 + b^3 = (a + b)(a^2 - ab + b^2)$

$a^3 - b^3 = (a - b)(a^2 + ab + b^2)$

Quadratic Formula

For $ax^2 + bx + c = 0$,

$x = \dfrac{-b \pm \sqrt{b^2 - 4ac}}{2a}$

Interest

Simple interest Formula:

$I = prt$

Interest Formula (compounded n times per year):

$A = p\left(1 + \dfrac{r}{n}\right)^{nt}$

A = Amount after t years.

p = principal

r = annual interest rate

t = time in years

I = Interest

Trigonometric Identities

Pythagorean Theorem: $a^2 + b^2 = c^2$

$\sin\theta = \dfrac{opp}{hyp}$

$\cos\theta = \dfrac{adj}{hyp}$

$\tan\theta = \dfrac{opp}{adj}$

$\sin^2\theta + \cos^2\theta = 1$

$Density = \dfrac{Mass}{Volume}$

Central Angle

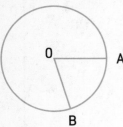

$$m\angle AOB = m\widehat{AB}$$

Inscribed Angle

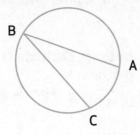

$$m\angle ABC = \frac{1}{2}m\widehat{AC}$$

Intersecting Chords Theorem

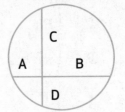

$$A \cdot B = C \cdot D$$

Probability

Permutations: $\quad _nP_r = \dfrac{n!}{(n-r)!}$

Combinations: $\quad _nC_r = \dfrac{n!}{(n-r)!r!}$

Multiplication rule (independent events): $\quad P(A \text{ and } B) = P(A) \cdot P(B)$

Multiplication rule (general): $\quad P(A \text{ and } B) = P(A) \cdot P(B|A)$

Addition rule: $\quad P(A \text{ or } B) = P(A) + P(B) - P(A \text{ and } B)$

Conditional Probability: $\quad P(B|A) = \dfrac{P(A \text{ and } B)}{P(A)}$

Arithmetic Sequence: $\quad a_n = a_1 + (n-1)d$ where a_n is the nth term, a_1 is the first term, and d is the common difference.

Geometric Sequence: $\quad a_n = a_1 r^{(n-1)}$ where a_n is the nth term, a_1 is the first term, and r is the common ratio.

Order of Operations	The TI-30XS MultiView™ automatically evaluates numerical expressions using the Order of Operations based on how the expression is entered.	The correct answer is 23.

Example
$12 \div 2 \times 3 + 5 =$

Note that the 2 is **not** multiplied by the 3 before division occurs.

Decimals	To calculate with decimals, enter the whole number, then [.], then the fractional part.	The correct answer is 17.016.

Example
$11.526 + 5.89 - 0.4 =$

The decimal point helps line up the place value.

Fractions	To calculate with fractions, use the $\frac{n}{d}$ button. The answer will automatically be in its simplest form.	The correct answer is $\frac{15}{28}$.

Example
$\frac{3}{7} \div \frac{4}{5} =$

This key combination works if the calculator is in Classic mode or MathPrint™ mode.

Mixed Numbers	To calculate with mixed numbers, use the [2nd] $\frac{n}{d}$ button. To see the fraction as an improper fraction, don't press the [2nd] [×10ⁿ] buttons in sequence below.	The correct answer is $39\frac{13}{15}$.

Example
$8\frac{2}{3} \times 4\frac{3}{5} =$

8 [2nd] $\frac{n}{d}$ 2 [▼] 3 [enter] [×] 4 [2nd] $\frac{n}{d}$ 3 [▼] 5 [enter] [2nd] [×10ⁿ] [enter]

This key combination only works if the calculator is in MathPrint™ mode.

Percentages	To calculate with percentages, enter the percent number, then [2nd] [( ].	The correct answer is 360.

Example
$72\% \times 500 =$

7 2 [2nd] [( ] [×] 5 0 0 [enter]

Powers & Roots

To calculate with powers and roots, use the (x^2) and

(∧) buttons for powers and the (2nd) (x^2) and (2nd)

(∧) buttons for roots.

Example
$21^2 =$

[2] [1] (x^2) (enter)

The correct answer is 441.

Example
$2^8 =$

[2] (∧) [8] (enter)

The correct answer is 256.

Example
$\sqrt{729} =$

(2nd) (x^2) [7] [2] [9] (enter)

The correct answer is 27.

Example
$\sqrt[5]{16807} =$

[5] (2nd) (∧) [1] [6] [8] [0] [7] (enter)

The correct answer is 7.

You can use the (2nd) (x^2) and (2nd) (∧) buttons to also compute squares and square roots.

Scientific Notation

To calculate in scientific notation, use the (×10ⁿ) button as well as make sure your calculator is in Scientific notation in the (mode) menu.

The correct answer is 1.2011×10^5.

Example
$6.81 \times 10^4 + 5.201 \times 10^4 =$

[6] [.] [8] [1] (×10ⁿ) [4] (enter) (+)

[5] [.] [2] [0] [1] (×10ⁿ) [4] (enter)

When you are done using scientific notation, make sure to change back to Normal in the (mode) menu.

Toggle

In MathPrint™ mode, you can use the toggle button (◄►) to switch back and forth from exact answers (fractions, roots, π, etc.) and decimal approximations.

The correct answer is 0.428571429.

Example
$\frac{3}{7} =$

[3] (n/d) [7] (enter) (◄►)

If an exact answer is not required, you can press the toggle button (◄►) immediately to get a decimal approximation from an exact answer without reentering the expression.